AF269649

The Art of Trumpet Teaching

John Keith Johnson (1942–2020).
Courtesy of Cecile Johnson.

The Art of Trumpet Teaching

The Legacy of Keith Johnson

Leigh Anne Hunsaker

North Texas Lives of Musicians Series Number 16

University of North Texas Press
Denton, Texas

Permissions:
University of North Texas Press
1155 Union Circle #311336
Denton, TX 76203-5017

The paper used in this book meets the minimum requirements of the
American National Standard for Permanence of Paper for Printed Library
Materials, z39.48.1984. Binding materials have been chosen for durability.

Library of Congress Cataloging-in-Publication Data

Hunsaker, Leigh Anne, author. | Stowman, William, writer of foreword.
  The art of trumpet teaching : the legacy of Keith Johnson / Leigh Anne
Hunsaker.
    pages cm
  Includes bibliographical references and index.
  ISBN-13 978-1-57441-858-3 (cloth)
  ISBN-13 978-1-57441-869-9 (ebook)
  1. LCSH: Trumpet—Instruction and study. 2. Johnson, Keith, 1942–2020.
3. Music teachers—United States—Biography.

  MT440 .H85 2022
  788.9/2193--dc23
                        2021061594

The Art of Trumpet Teaching is Number 16 in the
North Texas Lives of Musicians Series

International Trumpet Guild Journal articles reprinted by permission.

The electronic edition of this book was made possible by the support of the
Vick Family Foundation. Typeset by vPrompt eServices.

For my parents,
Michael and Carolyn Hunsaker,
who have supported my endeavors with
love and good humor.

Contents

Foreword

Take a big breath and make a beautiful sound. I can't tell you how many times Keith said that to me. But it was a lot. And I never got tired of it. It was his way. It was comforting, informative, reassuring … and in an instant those words brought the kind of peace one needs to relax, to be at his best, and to play music beautifully.

Take a big breath and make a beautiful sound. With this one phrase, whether stated in a lesson or just before I walked onstage to play a recital, he delivered me to a quiet place where I could do all the things he taught me. And even when I moved on and he was no longer by my side, I could still hear it—auditions, concerts, recordings, it didn't matter. I can hear it right now as I type these words.

Take a big breath and make a beautiful sound. This has come to mean more to me with each passing year. It was his way of taking all music-making, all life really, and putting it into one simple phrase. It was his masterful way of reminding us that no matter what we face, we take it in and then strive to be as beautiful as we can be—with our trumpet, our loved ones, our students, in our profession, and in life.

Take a big breath and make a beautiful sound. This was his way of putting into words what he did as a teacher for so many years, for so many people, in so many ways. He was caring and demanding. He was patient and relentless. He was brilliant and funny. And as much as he loved playing his trumpet, it was never really about the trumpet. It was always about people.

Take a big breath and make a beautiful sound. This phrase allowed me to leave every lesson feeling like Superman, to walk onstage with confidence and gratitude, and to work each day to become the teacher he would want me to be. And now, those words help us endure the loss of a wonderful man, a master teacher, a friend whose only compass was artistic true north. And while sharing these thoughts helps ease the pain a bit, what I intend to do to honor my teacher, mentor, and friend is exactly what he taught me to do …

"Take a big breath and make a beautiful sound."

William Stowman
Messiah University

Preface

I first read Keith Johnson's celebrated book, *The Art of Trumpet Playing*, when I was a teenager and immediately decided that I had to study with him. But for a kid from southern Oklahoma, the University of Northern Iowa seemed impossibly remote. Several years later after college and a few years of teaching, I met Keith Johnson after his clinic at the 1988 Texas Music Educators Association conference. Johnson had recently accepted the job at North Texas and soon afterwards I began graduate study there.

My notes from my first lesson with him read, "Mr. Johnson is a lot like I thought he would be—just like his book. He is very relaxed and not in a hurry about anything." During that hour he described his concept of teaching and began my initiation into his distinctive pedagogical approach.

I was a member of Johnson's studio for three years and continued to stay in touch and perform with him after completing my Ph.D. at North Texas. When he announced his retirement, I began planning this book project, envisioning a compilation of his pedagogical ideas as experienced by members of his studio.

When tributes from former students began arriving, however, many of them were descriptions of their close relationship with Johnson and expressions of their appreciation for his kindness and guidance. Despite my hints that I would like people to describe their experiences with his teaching, it soon became apparent that their outpouring of love and gratitude focused on the unique relationship that each had felt with him.

Upon reflection, that seems perfectly appropriate. One of the points that Johnson repeatedly stressed in his pedagogy classes and in virtually every conversation about teaching was, "We are *not* teaching the instrument; we are teaching the person." His colleague Adam Gordon remarked, "He not only taught you guys how to play—he taught you how to be." With the help of many colleagues and former students, this book is a portrait of the man who has been not only an artist teacher but also a mentor and friend to many.

Many contributors have shared cherished personal memories and insights for this book, and it could not have been written without their help. Their stories are much appreciated, and I am sure that there are many more to be told. Every attempt was made to contact former Johnson students from the universities of Northern Iowa and North Texas, and no slight is intended toward anyone who was inadvertently overlooked. At this writing, no master list exists of all his students, but after Keith Johnson's six decades of college teaching, surely our name is Legion.

Trevor Duell graciously allowed me the use of his unpublished interview with Keith Johnson, which he recorded on February 15, 2014. This contains a great deal of Johnson's background information and personal history, which would not now be available without Trevor's project and his generosity in sharing it.

Keith's wife Cecile was instrumental in providing contacts and background information. She is a strong woman, a dedicated wife and mother, and an internationally known Kodály expert. Another book could be written about her, but perhaps Jason Bergman said it best:

> Cecile Johnson is the gem of the Johnson family. Her love and care for Keith is remarkable. She cares deeply about the UNT trumpet studio as well. In fact, any great studio or professional accomplishment one achieves is part of a partnership that makes it possible. Cecile worked for years to support Keith in his efforts to grow the UNT trumpet studio. Their teamwork impacted hundreds of trumpet students, as well as the lives of Keith's colleagues.

Many thanks to Dr. Laura Pogue, associate professor of English and W. D. and Hollis R. Bond Endowed Chair of English at Hardin Simmons University for reading the early draft with an eagle eye and offering encouragement and many helpful suggestions.

Dr. Anne Hardin, the patron saint of brass authors and former editor of the *International Trumpet Guild Journal*, was very helpful with editorial suggestions. A long-time friend of Keith Johnson, she agreed to advise on this project and became a supportive coach and a good friend.

Leigh Anne Hunsaker

Introduction

How does one document the legacy of a man whose influence as a performer, teacher, and author was so widespread? Keith Johnson has left us with an impressive array of professional accomplishments, but the most lasting part of his legacy may be the people he influenced. Johnson's former students speak of the life lessons he imparted and their far-reaching impact on their personal and professional lives. As one student described it, he not only taught us to sing through the horn, but also to sing through life.

The Art of Trumpet Teaching details the life and work of master teacher Keith Johnson from his boyhood through his tenure at the University of Northern Iowa (1966–1986) and the University of North Texas (1986–2014).

Part One, "Musician, Mentor, Master Teacher," describes the life and legacy of Keith Johnson through the words of former students and colleagues. Part Two, "Pedagogy," organizes his pedagogical concepts and broader principles for music study. Part Three, "Reflections," is a collection of tributes that honor his memory, and Part Four, "Articles," contains noteworthy writings by Johnson.

Keith Johnson Masterclass at Messiah University.
Courtesy of William Stowman.

Part One

Musician, Mentor, Master Teacher

Keith Johnson circa 1949.
Courtesy of Cecile Johnson.

Early Years

John Keith Johnson was born in Center, Texas on August 25, 1942. His father was a Marine in World War II, and in his early years he lived with his mother and her parents. His paternal grandparents and other relatives also lived in the same small town in East Texas. In an unpublished interview in 2014 with Trevor Duell, Johnson recalled early memories of his father:

> He was shipped off to the Pacific and didn't come home for well over three years. You went and stayed until the fighting was done. He didn't talk about it very much, but he was a rifle instructor and also taught some hand-to-hand combat. [His return] was kind of tough at first, because I was spoiled. I had four grandparents and a maiden aunt who just spoiled the dickens out of me! I remember the first time my dad told me to do something and I said, "No." One does not say that to a combat-scarred Marine. It probably took us twenty-three or twenty-four years to get things worked out. At that point I didn't need to ask him for money, so that improved the relationship.[1]

Keith's mother Maxine taught English and World History, and played piano and organ in the local Methodist church. Keith began piano lessons in the first grade for a couple of years and began to sing in both the children's choir and the adult choir while in grade school, because he greatly enjoyed the music of the Methodist church.

Johnson described his introduction to the school band program in the sixth grade:

> The music store and the band director came to school and had a show. For reasons that aren't really clear to me, I picked the cornet. I thought the flute was enticing because most of the people playing flute were girls and I thought, "Well, if I picked the flute, I might have a better shot at getting a date sometime." But I picked the cornet and I really don't know why. Part of it was that it was not as heavy as the trombone, or the euphonium, or the tuba. He chuckled. So, if I was going to play a brass instrument, I wanted one that wasn't going to require as much work. I just picked the cornet and took it home. It was $150 as I recall.
>
> My mom was an influence and she was a pretty good piano player. Dad had no musical training of any sort, and frankly I don't think he had any interest. I'm not sure he wouldn't have preferred I try out for the football team rather than the band. Since there were no girls on the football team, again band was the more attractive option!
>
> The first year I was in band I had a wonderful band director named Carroll Colvert, who was one of these people who could get everybody pumped up. Quite inspirational and a very, very nice man. Unfortunately, he left at the end of my first year, but then a man named Blanton McDonald became the band director. He was also very good. He was very hard working.[2]

Blanton McDonald, a spry ninety-three-year-old at this writing, was a highly regarded band director, and is a member of the National Association of Military Marching Bands Hall of Fame. McDonald encouraged Johnson to take private lessons, so he began studying with William Scarlato, the principal trumpet of the Shreveport Symphony. Johnson said this of Scarlato:

> What I remembered most was how pumped up I got to play the trumpet. One of the more interesting components of my work with him was that he often forgot my lessons. This may have had something to do with the way I played. I don't know. It was a sixty-mile

drive and it was a long sixty miles over bad roads. He taught at a Jesuit Boys School, I'd say about forty percent of the time he would forget, so I would just have to turn around and drive home. I'd call him when I got home and we'd set up a lesson for next time. He only charged three dollars, so even if I didn't get a lesson every time, it was okay.[3]

On one of these trips, Johnson heard his first orchestra, the Shreveport Symphony, performing an outdoor concert. "I was totally knocked out," Johnson remembered. At age seventeen, this experience led him to become a musician, although he did not know the name of the piece he had heard. Johnson described his background:

All I had played was band music. In the Fall we marched and in the Spring we sat down and played. There were no private lessons [in Center], there were no theory classes, no music history, no choral program, and no string program. And that was it, pretty basic. The thing I remembered most about that is the skill I developed as a sight reader. The band director would let me use his office with his file cabinets of all the music. I would pull out the file drawer for marches and read through the first cornet part of every piece. He must have had two or three hundred marches. I could work through the drawer and by the time I played through them all, I would just start over. I was put into the high school band when I was in seventh grade.[4]

Johnson graduated from Center High School in 1960 and immediately went to North Texas to study with John Haynie during the summer: "I graduated on a Friday night in May, and on Monday morning I was here [Denton] because I wanted to get into music!"[5] In the fall semester, Johnson began studying with a teaching fellow, but after a week Haynie had a vacancy, and Johnson studied with him for the next three years. He spent one semester as a music education major, then realized that he wanted to perform and teach individuals rather than be a band director. He received a bachelor of arts degree in music, with minors in English literature and German. He finished his degree in three years: "I wanted to get through it as quickly as I could so I could get to graduate school, which looked like a whole lot more fun.[6]

Keith Johnson, Center High School Band at age 14 in 1956.
Courtesy of Cecile Johnson.

Johnson described his trumpet study at North Texas saying:

Mr. Haynie's lessons had a lot to do with the physical aspects of playing. It was all good information. I think for the most part, I am still very comfortable with what he said. There was some analysis about embouchure and tongue placement; things of that sort were very prominent. I did everything he asked and I improved as a player. There were times when he was quite strict! I remember one time he said, "There are too many people missing notes around here. If you miss a note on an etude, you start over." I can remember playing one of the Charlier etudes; I don't remember which one, but it was damned hard. I got to the very last measure and I cracked a note. "Back to the top!"

Mr. Haynie's discipline was quite good. My teaching from a pedagogical standpoint is somewhat different from his. We went through tons of solo literature, tons of study materials. That was really wonderful. It was a very rich background. Then there were even more trumpet players; I think there were one hundred and sixty. There were eight or nine teaching fellows. I graduated a little frustrated because I wanted to do more orchestral playing.[7]

During his time at North Texas, Johnson took a few lessons on orchestral excerpts from Ron Modell, who was then the principal trumpet of the Dallas Symphony. He also played in the school orchestra, and formed a close relationship with the conductor:

There was an orchestra here and it was a pretty good one. It was run by a man named George Morey—a great musician, a fabulous flute player, and he also conducted the orchestra. This man was a genius; the brains were just popping out of his ears. He liked me; we got to be good friends. One summer, Dr. Morey was without a car and I was taking heavy course loads. I had a 7:00 a.m. Texas Government class. George Morey had a 7:00 a.m. class on Wagner, of all things. He asked if I could give him a ride to school and I did. It was probably the reason I made such good grades during the summer, because going to class at 7:00 in the morning was probably something I wouldn't have done.

Dr. Morey was a wonderful influence because I got to play for him in the orchestra. He gave me a piece of music as a thank you for driving him to school. It's a piece called "Le Fanfaron de La Fanfare" by Malipiero. He was a contemporary of Respighi. They were both highly responsible for bringing out the works of Vivaldi. Anyway, it's a wonderful piece for trumpet and piano: "the fanfare of fanfares." Dr. Morey had signed the cover, "Keith, Wagner and I could not have made it through the summer without you!"[8]

After finishing his degree at North Texas in 1963, Johnson began his graduate studies. He was accepted at the University of Illinois and the University of Michigan. He chose Illinois, in part because of John Haynie's connections at that school. Haskell Sexton had been Haynie's trumpet teacher, and the band director, Mark Hindsley, was Haynie's father-in-law.

Johnson recalled Sexton as "an absolute saint." Johnson and a roommate shared a house next door to Sexton, who would come over at night, eat popcorn, and watch the Johnny Carson show with them. Many of Johnson's students have heard the story of his first lesson with Sexton: "I went in and started to play and I was so nervous. After the third attempt, Mr. Sexton reached over, put his hand on my shoulder and said, 'This is Illinois, not North Texas, and I'm not John Haynie. I know he was a very demanding teacher. We do things differently here. Put your trumpet in your case and let's go to Prims [a local bar] and have a beer.' This was at 2:00 in the afternoon. That was my first lesson."[9]

Johnson remembered Sexton as being very generous and helpful in getting him playing jobs and students to teach. In his second year of study, Sexton told Johnson that he had made a great deal of progress in his playing and recommended that he go to Chicago and study with Vincent Cichowicz. Sexton arranged the first lesson for him, and this was the beginning of Johnson's immersion into the "Chicago School" of brass playing that guided his playing and teaching for the rest of his career.

After finishing his master's degree in 1965, Johnson had several teaching job offers and won the audition for the principal trumpet opening in the Honolulu Symphony. After arriving in Hawaii, he lived on a boat for two weeks and found that the contract and job were not as described. By the time he got back to the mainland, the other jobs had been filled, so he called John Haynie for advice. Haynie needed a teaching fellow and invited Johnson to return to North Texas. Johnson agreed and spent a year in the Ph.D. program in musicology.

At the end of that school year, Johnson received job offers from California State Fullerton, the University of Tulsa, and the University of Northern Iowa. He chose Iowa: "UNI appealed to me the most because it was in a small city with an orchestra."[10]

Chicago Influence

K eith Johnson often said, "We all stand on the shoulders of giants," and for him, as well as many other brass players, those giants were members of the Chicago Symphony brass section. Johnson began studying with Vincent Cichowicz (CSO second trumpet) while in Illinois and returned to Chicago for lessons during his year in the doctoral program at North Texas. He described his first lesson with Cichowicz:

Boy, that was it! The dark clouds parted! I learned so much in one hour. The whole approach—what I teach you—came out of that school. Just to hear him play was worth it. I started playing and I was very nervous and he said "Good playing is easy; you take a deep breath and you sing through the horn." Then he played a flow study for me. I have never heard a sound that beautiful. His sound on the trumpet was singularly the most beautiful trumpet playing. I know players who have greater upper register and maybe a little more technique—and he was pretty strong in all those areas—but as far as just playing a gorgeous sound is concerned, that's what I hear every morning when I warm up. I think about what he sounded like and I try to make that sound. It hasn't happened yet, but I'm getting closer![11]

Johnson continued studying with Cichowicz while teaching in Iowa and began to work with two other Chicago Symphony legends, Adolph Herseth (trumpet) and Arnold Jacobs (tuba). Johnson studied with Herseth on a few occasions and had numerous lessons with Jacobs over several years:

> A lesson with him was quite an experience. With Jacobs, he could pinpoint a problem and really go in right after it and fix it. There was never a problem for which he didn't have an immediate and direct solution. It was always correct. He knew his stuff; the man was a genius.
>
> He often did in a lesson whatever it was he wanted to do that day. It was never less than enormously valuable. Whatever musical or intellectual "meal" he prepared, it was more than worth consuming!
>
> I remember in the first lesson that I played something, and he said, "Well, you sound very good. Are there any particular areas you would like to work on?" To which I expressed interest in all the knowledge and research he had done on breathing. "Well, there's nothing wrong with the way you breathe except you're lazy; take a big breath! And don't forget to leave the $100 check."
>
> He would occasionally remind me to put more "Hollywood" into my playing, which of course meant more color and showing off. I finally learned to write everything down after a lesson with him. It was always little short things that I would write into my music: "sing this first," "take a fuller breath," "sit tall." Sometimes he would get off on a tangent, not in a bad sense, but he would go into some of the physiology of playing, perhaps because he knew I had done some writing.[12]

Johnson continued to coach with other orchestral musicians, including two of the principal trumpet players in the Boston Symphony Orchestra, Armando Ghitalla and Charles Schlueter. Of Ghitalla, Johnson said:

> I think I had three or four private lessons with him. At that point, I was in my early forties. I just loved being around him so much. He was a wonderful person who was full of life. You felt as though you were the center of his world. Cichowicz was much the same way. All my lessons with Ghitalla were in his summer house in Tanglewood.
>
> He was very helpful in the sense that he encouraged me to take lots of risks. He was a very flashy player and it was very interesting to hear him. He would play some solo that we all knew and it was never what you

expected. He always tweaked it and changed it. Sometimes it worked and it was so beautiful and other times it didn't work. He was unintimidated. If he missed a note, it was no big deal! He just went right on.

I asked him one time how he dealt with conductors. They are always different. Some are pretty secure and fun to work with while others aren't so secure and take it out on [the musicians]. He said, "I'll tell you what helps. When your hair starts turning gray, don't dye it. If you have gray hair and you look directly at the conductor and you don't blink and don't smile, chances are he'll leave you alone! Just never smile." He would do things like that.

One time I was playing the Arutunian [Concerto] for him. Down at the bottom of the first page, there is that lick that goes from g-flat to f to a-flat back to g-flat. For me, it's really tricky. My third finger is kind of dumb. I played it for him several times and cracked it each time. He leaned over very close and started whispering as if there were a microphone hidden somewhere and said, "If you won't tell anyone, I played this piece with Arthur [Fiedler] many times and I can never get that g-flat to work. Just play it g-natural. Arthur never caught it. If you can't do it, just bluff your way through!" It's the old "if you're getting run out of town by a mob, get out in front of them and act like you are leading the parade."[13]

While at the University of Northern Iowa, Johnson studied with Charles Schlueter, principal trumpet in Minneapolis. After he relocated to the University of North Texas, Johnson again worked with Schlueter, now principal trumpet of the Boston Symphony Orchestra. Johnson had great respect for Schlueter and brought him to UNT for trumpet masterclasses.

Keith Johnson and Charles Schlueter at ITG Conference in 2012.
Courtesy of Dave Monette.

New Hampshire Music Festival

I n 1964, while a graduate student at the University of Illinois, Johnson was encouraged by a friend to send an audition tape for a summer position at the New Hampshire Music Festival. The Music Director, Tom Nee, was the associate conductor of the Minneapolis Symphony. The Festival had begun in 1952 with a shoestring budget and an eight-week season for a small chamber orchestra. During the early years, the musicians were not paid, but received room and board and enjoyed the recreational opportunities of the lakes and mountains.

In the late 1960s, the Festival began paying the musicians and shortened the season to six weeks. Currently, the NHMF has a five-week season in July and August, including orchestra concerts, chamber ensembles, and choral music.

Johnson considered the New Hampshire Music Festival to be one of the most important influences in his professional and personal life. He met his future wife there and formed long-lasting relationships with many musicians and local residents. Johnson's students have been regaled with tales of both the musical and other activities in the NHMF.

A favorite story is how he met Cecile LeBlanc at the Music Festival, where her parents managed the musicians' housing. Cecile remembers meeting Keith in 1964, after her junior year in high school. She was working as a chambermaid at the music festival and recalls that "he drove a very spiffy maroon convertible." They got to know each other during the summers, and in 1969 after Cecile finished college things got serious.

That summer, Cecile was working as a waitress at The Old Oaken Bucket in Westford, Massachusetts. Keith and trombonist Dave Richie were on their way to Mary Rasmussen's house to view her collections of brass music and instruments and stopped at the Bucket for lunch. After the meal, when they were on the road again, Keith suddenly said, "I'm going to marry that girl!" and drove back to the restaurant. He invited Cecile to the music festival the following week, and she agreed to come. The concert was on Saturday night, and he proposed on Sunday. Cecile accepted but did not tell her parents until the following spring. Keith and Cecile continued their secret long-distance courtship for a year and were married on June 27, 1970 at St. Ann's Church in Littleton, Massachusetts. Reflecting on their fifty-year marriage in conversation with the author, Cecile recalled her early work as a maid and a waitress and said, "My job status didn't change a lot, but the benefits of marriage were much better!"

The New Hampshire Music Festival became the summer home for the Johnsons as well as many other orchestra members. The relationship between the townspeople and the musicians was unique. The Festival enjoys strong support from the local population and summer residents, who work tirelessly to make the festival successful. There are many collaborations between local businesses and the musicians—coffee klatches with a brass trio at the Café Monte Alto are a favorite. The "Hut Concerts" of the 1970s have become an annual "Music in the Mountains" series, in which the public is invited to join musicians on a hike or walk in the Lakes Region of New Hampshire. These free events include light refreshments and an outdoor chamber concert at the peak or other destination of the excursion.

Trombonist David Loucky of Middle Tennessee State University began playing in the festival in 1987 and enjoys the family atmosphere and the high quality of music making in beautiful surroundings. Musicians and their families were housed in dorms, which allowed much camaraderie and interaction on a daily basis. Loucky said, "I like to think of it as an indoor camping experience. There is a family-centered atmosphere and a type of closeness that you don't get in a full-time orchestra."[14]

Many musicians are university teachers during the year and enjoy the chance for full-time music-making in the summer. Other Festival performers, such as tuba player Roger Bobo, have established full-time performing careers. Johnson's colleagues in the trumpet section have included Allan Dean, Tom Lisenbee, Jay Lichtmann, John McElroy, and Jason Bergman.

Keith treasured the musical and personal relationships and enjoyed recruiting other musicians to the NHMF, including violinist Kristin van Cleve, who described her first year at the Festival:

> My husband Mike and I first attended the New Hampshire Music Festival almost twenty years ago at the invitation of Keith Johnson. Keith himself was a longtime member of the festival, attending for over forty years without missing a summer. The festival, set in the beautiful New England town of Plymouth, New Hampshire, embodies those characteristics I always associate with Keith—high artistic standards combined with gracious collegiality.
>
> During our first summer, with his typical gentlemanly style, Keith ushered us around the beautiful lakes of central New Hampshire, showing us his favorite sights and taking us to his favorite restaurants. NHMF is indeed unique—the musicians feel a sense of pride in the music they produce every summer, as well as a real connection to the community. Music is made, friendships are formed that last for decades, and children of the musicians grow up experiencing the festival every summer, preparing the next generation. We owe a debt of gratitude to Keith Johnson for setting the tone for so many years.[15]

The summer gig that Johnson began playing in graduate school became one of the most lasting and significant parts of his life. In a letter to friends and family dated August 18, 2013, he wrote:

> Last Thursday, August 15, was a memorable event in my life, and you were so kind to be a part of the celebration of my fifty years with the New Hampshire Music Festival. It is difficult to find words to express what an impact the Festival has had on my life. Without the Festival

it is unlikely that I would ever have met Cecile, or that our children would have had the opportunities they encountered during those many wonderful summers in New Hampshire.

I have also been fortunate to play in a fine orchestra with superb colleagues, many of whom remain lifelong friends.[16]

Keith Johnson remains the longest tenured musician at the NHMF, retiring after fifty-three years. The Johnson family now endows the orchestra's trumpet section.

Faith and Family

When visiting the Johnsons recently, I noticed the array of items on Keith's bedside table. Unlike his study, which was packed with trumpet music, academic books, and recordings, this was his treasure trove of personal items—pictures of family members and books on spiritual matters and parenting. Faith and family were the underpinnings of Johnson's life.

Many who knew Keith Johnson personally noticed a centered, spiritual dimension to his personality. As an undergraduate student at North Texas, Johnson was involved with the Canterbury Episcopal Student Ministry. There he met Father Emmett Waits, the priest at St. Barnabas Episcopal Church in Denton and chaplain of the college ministry. The two formed a close friendship that lasted the rest of Father Waits' life. In Johnson's book, *The Art of Trumpet Playing*, he expresses "deepest gratitude … to Father Emmett Waits, who taught me to appreciate beauty, order, and mystery."

The Johnsons also named their son after Father Waits. As Johnson shared the conversation, he called his friend, saying, "Father, we have a son, and we named him after you." The priest's response was, "Oh no! You didn't!" He was only slightly relieved to hear that the baby's full name was Stephen Gordon Waits Johnson.

The Johnson Family.
Courtesy of Cecile Johnson.

Courtesy of Cecile Johnson.

Courtesy of Cecile Johnson.

Through his association with Canterbury, Johnson joined St. Barnabas and loved serving in the Episcopal Church. He had a great appreciation for the marriage of the liturgy and music that enhances the service. Johnson was very devout and often said that if he had not been a trumpet player, he would have been a late-vocation deacon, a servant ministry. Faith was embedded in his life.

While in Iowa Keith and Cecile adopted two "Gerber babies." Andrea was born in Center, Texas in 1976 and was delivered by the same doctor who delivered Keith. Keith's mother and uncle were instrumental in arranging the adoption, although Keith's mother passed away three months before Andrea was born. Stephen was adopted through Catholic Charities. Born in March 1978, he was received by Cecile in August while Keith was still performing in the New Hampshire Music Festival.

Both children spent their summers growing up with Festival musicians and with Cecile's family on the East Coast. Andrea and Stephen both studied piano and violin, although neither chose to become a musician. Stephen was the first in the family to perform in Carnegie Hall, however, on a concert tour with his high school orchestra.

Today, Andrea is a second grade teacher in Texas. Her daughter Victoria is a nursing student at Texas Tech University. Stephen received a degree in Criminal Justice from the University of North Texas. He worked as a police officer for several years and is now a compliance officer and fraud investigator for J. P. Morgan Chase in San Antonio.

Cecile Johnson played clarinet through college. After marriage she decided that one practicing musician in the family was enough. She concentrated on classroom music teaching in Billerica, Massachusetts and taught junior high school choir in Waterloo and Cedar Falls, Iowa. She earned a master's degree in music education from the University of Northern Iowa, where Keith was the trumpet teacher. Professionally, the relocation to Texas in 1986 proved to be pivotal for both Keith and Cecile.

Cecile began teaching music at Woodrow Wilson Elementary School in Denton and became interested in the Kodály teaching philosophy. She completed her Kodály Master Teacher Certification at UNT in a program endorsed by the American Organization of Kodály Educators.

The music program at Woodrow Wilson flourished under Cecile's guidance. In addition to her classroom curriculum, she established the All-Star Choir, which commissioned more than thirty children's choir compositions. Her ensemble was a selected Texas Music Educators Association Elementary Honor Choir three times: in 1999, 2005, and 2011. She taught at Woodrow Wilson for twenty-five years, from 1986–2012 and was twice named teacher of the year.

Cecile has presented numerous workshops and clinics across the United States and visited Hungary on three separate pedagogy tours. She served as President of the Kodály Educators of Texas and as Southern Division President of the Organization of American Kodály Educators, and she also chaired two national OAKE conferences, in 2002 and 2012. She has recently retired from teaching in summer Kodály training institutes and is an adjunct professor in the UNT College of Music.

When asked how he balanced his career and family, Johnson replied: "I have to be honest. It has been very difficult. I suppose like all parents, there are things I wish I could go back and do over again. I really wish I had spent more time with my children. All the traveling I did to recruit students to try and build up my reputation and the reputation of the schools I worked for took a lot of time and energy. The thing that made it possible is that I have a wife who had a very good career in music."[17]

Over the years, students saw firsthand the importance he placed on family. Many of Johnson's students heard him talk about his two children and parenting in general. Quite simply, he loved being a father and family was his foundation. Nicholas Daugherty, a former student at Northern Iowa remembers:

> My girlfriend (now my wife of thirty-two years) and I would babysit Andrea and Stephen. On one such occasion, Keith said, "Oh don't worry, I got the kids a movie." It was a documentary about an otter, and it kept them occupied for about eight minutes!
>
> Sue and I treasure those times watching Keith and Cecile, as husband and wife, and as parents. Few people get to have that kind of relationship with a professor and his wife and family. It was such a great blessing for a kid who came from a divorced home and didn't have a lot of examples. What a treasure Keith was, and of course Cecile![18]

Instrument maker Dave Monette met Johnson through a repair job and the two forged a long and close friendship. Monette also remarked on the importance of faith and family in Johnson's life:

> I met Keith and Cecile almost forty years ago when I was working as an instrument repairman in Salem, Oregon. Keith sent me his B-flat and C trumpets to be rebuilt … and hopefully improved! Keith was pleased with the work and invited me to visit Cedar Falls to work with him and his students in person.
>
> This visit was the beginning of a friendship that included many memorable visits to Denton, where I was always their houseguest. Keith made many visits to my Chicago shop, and later Keith and the entire family visited me in Portland, Oregon, where I have lived and worked for almost thirty years now. Both children were a joy to be around as they were growing up. I especially remember meaningful conversations with Stephen as he entered young adulthood and was navigating career choice options and more. The integrity and inner moral compass Andrea and Stephen both bring to their family and career life are a lovely reflection on how they were raised.
>
> While Keith and I shared a deep love for the trumpet, much of our time together over the years was spent sharing our life's passions beyond the music world. We loved talking politics together, given that our views on so much were virtually identical. Many nights were spent at the Johnson table lamenting about events in Washington over a bowl of Keith's obligatory and much beloved "Blue Bell" ice cream! But it was our interactions over subjects much more important and personal than politics that I recall most vividly.
>
> Keith and I shared an outing to Dallas together years ago. He wanted to introduce me to his mentor at the Episcopal church—a man he admired greatly, Father Emmett Waits. We had a lovely time over lunch, visiting with Father Waits and talking about church life, personal lessons we were experiencing, and more. It was obvious Keith shared a remarkably strong bond with him and seemed to enjoy bringing the two of us together.
>
> This visit brought home for me the depth of Keith's passion not only for the ritual aspect of church ceremony, but also the human connection to a spiritual practice that directly impacted both his personal life and his interactions with students.[19]

Dave Monette and Keith Johnson.
Courtesy of Dave Monette.

The Northern Brass Quintet in 1975: (*from left to right*) Keith Johnson, Jon Hansen, Donald Little, David Kennedy, and Bruce Chidester. *Courtesy of Donald Little.*

University of Northern Iowa

Johnson began his full-time college teaching career in 1966 at State College of Iowa, now the University of Northern Iowa. He appreciated the close-knit atmosphere, and even shared dinner with the university president and his wife during his first week in Cedar Falls. In his first year, he taught trumpet and trombone, as well as a music theory class that caused him considerable concern: "I was scared to death! I actually broke out into a rash, I was so nervous! I got into the theory class and quickly discovered it wasn't nearly as bad as I had thought. Within two days, the rash was gone. So I just recruited like the devil and the next year I had a full load of students. I never had to teach theory again. I'm sure they were as happy about that as I was."[20]

Johnson also created courses in brass pedagogy and brass literature. His book, *The Art of Trumpet Playing*, came from his course outlines. UNI horn professor Thomas Tritle recalled:

Keith was an absolutely remarkable colleague. I came to UNI from Rio de Janeiro, where I had played co-principal for five years with the Brazilian Symphony. As a university professor, I was about as green as you could get, and Keith was a great model. He and Cecile were a class act—separately and together. He left the egotistical aspects of professorship aside and focused on the essentials necessary for each student to become a better trumpet player. Anyone can see how this approach culminated in his book, right down to the basics. I benefited greatly from the book myself.[21]

Another colleague, tuba player Donald Little, formed a long friendship and working relationship with Johnson that lasted nearly fifty years.

> I first met Keith and Cecile Johnson in Cedar Falls, Iowa in 1972 when I auditioned and interviewed for a graduate tuba position at the University of Northern Iowa. After driving into Cedar Falls from Chicago, I stayed with them at their beautiful Victorian-style home not far from downtown. I was immediately comfortable with Keith and Cecile, and I remember conversations about Chicago Symphony brass musicians and other musical things. We had so much in common, or, at the very least, he made me feel that way.
>
> I formally auditioned with the Northern Brass Quintet at the University of Northern Iowa the next morning. Keith's playing confirmed that we had much in common when I heard him warm-up on some Vincent Cichowicz flow studies with an immediately-recognizable warm and full characteristic sound similar to my Northwestern University trumpet colleagues who had studied with Mr. Cichowicz.
>
> Although I was not successful that day, I auditioned and interviewed again one year later for the first full-time tuba position at the University of Northern Iowa and was awarded the position. The following Fall 1973 was the beginning of a wonderful personal and professional relationship with Keith Johnson.[22]

While at UNI, Johnson was principal trumpet in the Waterloo/Cedar Falls Symphony and performed with the Northern Brass Quintet. This group was founded in 1968 and performed concerts and lecture-demonstrations in public schools and communities across the state. Trombone professor Jon Hansen, who worked with Johnson at UNI for seventeen years, recalled: "As performers in the Northern Brass Quintet, we were involved in some four hundred programs, including concerts and lecture/recitals. Over the years, Keith and I disagreed and argued over a great many subjects, but never music. Keith's knowledge of literature—solo, ensemble, and orchestral—was vast. He was a consummate musician."[23]

Tom Tritle said this of Johnson and the NBQ:

> It was a pleasure to work with him in the Northern Brass Quintet. This group attained a very high level from time to time, much of it due to Keith's organizational skills. Our constant travel to Iowa secondary schools had much to do with the recruiting success of the School of Music during his tenure. For many years I was on the road every Friday and performed in a good number of the high schools in the state.
>
> The story about the NBQ I most enjoy telling is about his long-time colleague, trumpet professor Bruce Chidester. I had discovered one of those turn-of-the-century "opera houses" in the little Iowa town with the strange name of What Cheer. This dot on the road in south central Iowa had been a coal mining community and had devolved into a sleepy backwater shopping location for area farmers. The ancient opera house, a relic of better times, occasionally opened its doors for a country music performance. I decided it would be a wonderful experience for the NBQ to play there and talked them into it. I think the other quintet members knew how it would turn out.
>
> Before the show started, Bruce decided to get some refreshment at the good-old-boys' bar across the street. Dressed in his tux and bow tie, he wandered into the bar, stopping all conversation immediately, and in a loud voice asked the bartender, "Can I have a glass of milk?" He was served such, and in the rapt silence, heard from the back of the bar an astonished outburst, "Jee-sus ... Christ!" Bruce set down the glass, smiled at the befuddled regulars, and left. We had nine wonderful audience members at the concert; we were told we would have had more had it not been a good planting night.
>
> Our evening with Iowa's past proved to be more valuable for its memories than for what musical conquests we might have made.[24]

Some of Johnson's colleagues at the University of Northern Iowa also had a strong Chicago connection. Tuba professor Donald Little performed in the Chicago Civic Orchestra and studied with CSO tubist Arnold Jacobs at Northwestern University. Trombone professor Jon Hansen had also studied with Jacobs, as well as with Frank Crisafulli, CSO trombonist.

While at UNI, Johnson and his colleagues organized many brass events. One in 1973 brought together artists and composers including the New York Brass Quintet, John Swallow, Paul Ingraham, Harvey Phillips, Toby Hanks, and Halsey Stevens.[25]

Johnson had attended many masterclasses given by CSO principal trumpet
Adolph Herseth and tubist Arnold Jacobs and brought them to UNI:

> Herseth would come in for a number of workshops I hosted. It was
> like having a lesson but in some ways, almost better. Of course, he
> was very helpful. He really didn't teach so much as he coached and
> demonstrated. To hear him play was easily worth the cost! His teach-
> ing philosophies were very simple. "Just listen to it, think how it
> sounds and then play it." That's an oversimplification, but that was
> his message.
>
> Jacobs started his clinics by saying, "Don't analyze, take a big
> breath and sing! Song and wind!" Fifty-nine minutes later he would
> finish with that like adding a coda to reprise the introduction. In the
> middle he would demonstrate his vast knowledge of the physiology of
> respiration. It was really wonderful. It really was![26]

During his twenty years at UNI, Johnson developed a strong trumpet program.
He was very active as a performer and clinician, and *The Art of Trumpet Playing*
brought him national and international recognition. His former students in
Iowa mention the hallmarks that characterized Johnson's teaching career for
so long: excellent pedagogy, high standards, and his commitment to students.
UNI graduate Mark Duffy remembers:

> One of my earliest meetings with Keith was around Freshman Orien-
> tation, with my dad in tow. Let's just say that Pop had his doubts about
> this music major idea. Keith was a great help, and he had a similar story
> about his own dad's path to "believing I could make a living blowing
> on a hunk of brass!"
>
> Keith took a personal interest in his students, and no matter how
> serious you were about that hunk of brass, there was always time to
> find out how the campus life was going, or to recommend the best
> restaurant for a date before a Chicago Symphony concert.
>
> Keith also had a perspective on ensemble playing that I hadn't
> considered before. Having generally been the lead player, always
> counted on to take the high parts, it was new to have a teacher tell me
> that he was more about being a great second trumpet player. Maybe
> being the best reader in a trumpet section, or the one with the best time,
> or bringing one's best sound to the inner harmonies did more for the
> group than living for the stratosphere.

Although we had plenty of work to do in the trumpet playing endeavor, there was always time to wander off and discuss the bigger picture. One time we got on to architecture, and agreed we were jealous of the beauty of Iowa State's campus. Keith's impression of the neighboring Communication Arts building, with its dark halls of concrete: "My kids are afraid to go in there!"

Although Keith held a great respect for his fellow professors in the School of Music, he did admit to a little mischief at times. His pal, trombone professor Jon Hansen, often referred to a large blackboard in his own studio, which was covered in drawings of audio waveforms representing dynamic levels and articulations. Keith confessed to me more than once that he felt irresistibly compelled to sneak into the trombone studio and erase the whole thing. I don't know if he ever pulled that off.[27]

Nicholas Daugherty described his experience in Johnson's studio and classes:

Keith was so gracious to me as a young trumpet player. His steady push for me to improve with the ability to make me feel like I could reach the next level was priceless. He provided opportunities for me to play with the Waterloo/Cedar Falls Symphony.

Once, after stepping all over a section of a solo in a lesson, I said out loud, "Where was my head?" and Keith said, "In a very dark place." He would stand in the back of the room during solo performances and just look at me with encouraging eyes, and then take the recording and say, "You can't have this for thirty days; otherwise, you will only listen for the mistakes."

As an out-of-state student, he let me audit his Orchestral Excerpt class one summer so I could save some money. He never gave empty praise; you had to earn it, and that is what drove you to work. On the final exam we had several excerpts to play. When I finished the excerpt for Petrushka, he paused, and calmly looked at me and said, "I could not have played it better." I still carry those words with me over thirty years later.[28]

Johnson, always a committed teacher, was known for his disdain of university bureaucracy and administrators in general, although he spent a semester as Acting Director of the School of Music. He stated that he spent most of that time reading the *Wall Street Journal* and claimed to be unable to remember anything useful ever occurring in staff meetings. He told students,

"The only good thing about our faculty meetings was Margaret Merrion's coffee cake."[29]

Years later, Johnson described his studio at UNI: "When I was teaching in Iowa, the preponderance of my studio was students majoring in music education. Most of them were quite excited about becoming Iowa band directors. There were also a number of them that were serious trumpet players. Several of them got performance degrees. Many went on to play in military bands in D.C. They really kept me going and I must have been doing something right because John Haynie said, 'You sent me more graduate students than most other schools put together.'"[30]

Keith Johnson and Nicholas Daugherty at senior recital at
University of Northern Iowa in 1986.
Courtesy of Nick Daugherty.

University of
North Texas

During the 1984-85 school year, John Haynie announced his intention to enter a period of modified service, and a search for a new full-time trumpet professor was initiated. The search was not completed the first year, and Donald Little, who was now the tuba professor at North Texas, encouraged Johnson to apply. In 1986, Johnson was offered the position as a full professor with tenure and succeeded his former teacher, John Haynie. Organist and former professor at Northern Iowa, Jesse Eschbach, also took a position at North Texas that year and was very glad to make the transition at the same time as Johnson:

> We discovered in February that we were both under serious consideration. Following interviews in April, we were informed that we were hired. The long-distance lines were humming as we exchanged information about our respective moves to Texas, a state and culture that Keith knew and understood and of which I knew nothing.
>
> And thank heavens for Keith and me showing up together in the class of 1986, both hires of Mark Myers. Like most academic institutions, UNT was fraught with politics, and Keith provided me with counsel and advice that allowed me to weather the storms.

Had it not been for his wise words, I probably wouldn't have survived.

This brings me to the heart of the matter: Keith was invariably calm and reasoned in all that he undertook. He understood the system far better than the rest of us. He was always in demand for committee work, and invariably wound up chairing them.

His days were consumed not only with teaching a very large studio, practice, and performances throughout the metroplex, but also with very time-consuming searches. As soon as a new Provost, Dean, or University President was needed, Keith was on the job. It was his calm, reassuring, cultured personality, coupled with his strategic knowledge of bureaucracy that made him the "go to" person, especially for younger faculty negotiating the vicissitudes of UNT bureaucracy.[31]

While at North Texas, Johnson was instrumental in building the trumpet DMA program. Tuba professor Donald Little, who had come to North Texas in 1976, remarked that Johnson brought a different style of trumpet teaching to North Texas: "His studio quickly became the place to come for graduate trumpet study."[32] From 2003 through 2011, Johnson taught an average of fifteen doctoral students, six master's degree candidates, and up to four undergraduate students each semester.[33] In 2003, the North Texas DMA trumpet program was one of the largest in the nation with fifteen DMA candidates;[34] in 2004, there were seventeen.[35]

In his annual faculty update for 2005, Johnson wrote: "This past year has been the most demanding that I have experienced in forty years of full-time college teaching. The doctoral trumpet program at the University of North Texas, now the largest in the country, currently has twenty-three [DMA] students in progress, twenty of whom are my students."[36]

Dr. John Scott, clarinet professor and Chair of Instrumental studies, praised Johnson's record for graduate employment, saying, "He watched over his students, took care of them, and they got jobs. He was as successful as anyone I know in placing doctoral students."[37]

In addition to his record of placing graduates in university and orchestra positions, Keith Johnson developed a strong pipeline from his studio to leading military ensembles. One of the first of Johnson's students to enlist was

Keith Johnson and John Haynie in 2005.
Courtesy of Anne Hardin.

Susan Rider, member of "The President's Own" United States Marine Band, who began studying with Johnson while in high school:

> I studied with Keith from my sophomore year in high school through my freshman year at UNI. I have fond memories of having lessons during those high school days standing next to the washer and dryer in the basement as we worked through the concepts that would impact my future musical career. Many of these ideas came from the Chicago Symphony Orchestra brass section members Arnold Jacobs and Vincent Cichowicz. These philosophies were landmarks in Keith's teaching style. I was not always patient in my studies, but he was methodical and didn't rush things. Keith was teaching me another lesson through my naïve frustration during this time—that the mastery of becoming a musician and learning an instrument takes a lot of patience, time, and commitment.
>
> During my freshman year at UNI, Keith took a teaching position at North Texas. Although I stayed at UNI to complete my degree, Keith understood and supported me. As I continued my trumpet studies with Randy Grabowski, Charles Gorham and Edmund Cord, Keith's wisdom and guidance were reinforced and built upon time and time again through these other master teachers. His friendship and support of my career never wavered.[38]

Other Johnson students found careers in military ensembles: Nicholas Althouse, Robert Barnett, Marty Bishop, Ryan Brewer, Trevor Duell, Carl Eitzen, Jonas Feldman, Phillip Kennedy Johnson, John Manning, Brandon Potts, James Wood, and Ward Yager. Trevor Duell was one of the last Johnson students at North Texas:

> I was a student of Keith Johnson's from fall 2011 to spring 2014. He stayed on long enough to give my class of DMA students our three years of applied lessons. I am still unpacking everything I learned in those three years. Toward the end of my time in his studio, I had expressed some hesitation about finding a tenure track professorship. Many universities were still under hiring freezes, and the recession of 2008 kept numerous professors from retiring. He asked me if I had ever considered enlisting in a U.S. military band. I told him that going through basic training in my thirties was not exactly high on my list. Nevertheless, he insisted that I contact several of his former students who were currently serving and assured me that they were among his

most successful and active students. While he wouldn't speak for my ability to do push-ups, he thought that my temperament and character would fit in well.

After some careful consideration and encouragement from James Wood and Marty Bishop, I enlisted. I don't regret it for a single moment. I am very grateful to be able to use my time and talent to serve in the Army. I also look forward to the time when I can impart all his wisdom to other trumpeters as an instructor at the Army School of Music.[39]

While teaching at North Texas, Johnson began performing with the Dallas Opera, the Fort Worth Symphony, and the Sundance Brass, as well as the UNT faculty brass quintet and sextet. He also performed with the Dallas Symphony Orchestra, the Kansas City Orchestra, the Shreveport Symphony, Mexico City Philharmonic, and the Mexico City Symphony.

In the late 1990s, Johnson began to play the Baroque trumpet. During this time, the UNT Early Music Department was growing, and interest in studying the historic instrument increased among the trumpet students. Johnson took a professional development leave to study Baroque trumpet with Stephen Keavy and John Thiessen. He also researched early brass instruments with Robert Sheldon, the former curator of early instruments for the Smithsonian Institute and the Library of Congress. In March 2003, Johnson hosted a Baroque Trumpet Symposium at UNT, in which John Thiessen and Adam Gordon joined him as featured performers and clinicians. The two-day event included clinics and masterclasses on natural trumpet performance practice and pedagogy. Thiessen, Gordon, and Johnson performed with the UNT Baroque Orchestra, and Kathryn James (now Kathryn James Aducci) led the UNT Baroque Trumpet Ensemble.

Johnson also performed on Baroque trumpet with the Dallas Bach Society, Fort Worth Early Music, the Orchestra of New Spain, the San Francisco Bach Choir and Orchestra, Texas Baroque Trumpets, Texas Camerata, and the New York Baroque Orchestra.

Johnson was active in the International Trumpet Guild, serving as Music Review Editor from 1981 to 1988. He presented at many ITG conferences and was a cohost of the 1988 conference with Leonard Candelaria and John Haynie. Johnson also served three terms as a member of the Board of

Trevor Duell and Keith Johnson at the National Trumpet
Competition at the University of North Texas in 2018.
Courtesy of Trevor Duell.

From left to right: John Thiessen, Keith Johnson, and Adam Gordon.
Courtesy of Cecile Johnson.

Texas Baroque Trumpets: (*from left to right*) Jason Dovel, Nicholas
Althouse, Keith Johnson, Adam Gordon, and Leigh Anne Hunsaker.
Courtesy of Jason Dovel.

Directors of the International Trumpet Guild and received their Award of Merit in 2012 for service to the trumpet profession. Anne Hardin, former editor of the ITG Journal remembers their first meeting:

We met at the 1981 ITG Conference in Boulder, Colorado. In the early days of ITG, everyone played on the Festival of Trumpets concert, and rehearsals were scheduled around the clock. My rehearsal schedule said 11:30. I remember that because I'd been sitting in Mel Broiles' masterclass and knew I'd have to slip out. You didn't need a spread sheet then to know where to be when. Sessions were held one at a time; nothing overlapped. No one skipped anything, and getting up and leaving early was considered bad manners. But I had to make my rehearsal, and I hoped the members glaring at me assumed I had editorial business to attend to. As I headed toward the concert hall, I was joined by another trumpet player. He, too, was surprised that our rehearsal was scheduled during a prime-time lecture. Falling in step together we introduced ourselves. "Oh, you're the editor of the journal," he said. "I've just had a book published, and I'd love to have it reviewed in the Journal." "Sure. Send me a copy and I'll take care of it." We arrived at an empty auditorium, so we looked at our rehearsal schedules again. The 11:30 was correct, but the rehearsal was PM, not AM. "Well, how about a cup of coffee?" he asked. He talked about his new book, and what he was reading at the time. He asked about my work as a band director and the kind of books I liked. He said he'd like to help with the Journal.

Was this Fate? My music review editor Michael Tunnell had just taken over as Editor of General News. "Well, I need a music review editor. Would you be interested?" He accepted on the spot. It wasn't just that I needed a music review editor. I did. But my impression that he could handle the job perfectly was as spontaneous as it was correct. Every editor should have a Keith Johnson on staff. His columns were never late, they'd been meticulously edited, and he made everyone look good in print.

In 1982, Keith was the guest clinician and soloist with the Richland County Senior Honor Band. This was my teaching district, and I was responsible for choosing the junior honor band director—Claude Greever from Abingdon, Virginia, and the guest clinician/soloist—Keith Johnson. His masterclasses were stellar, and the band thought he hung the moon. The evening of the gala concert, he played the Erickson Trumpet Concerto on his C trumpet with the B-flat part on the stand. That did not go unnoticed by the trumpet section. It was a fabulous performance, and after much applause he came backstage. "That was just great!" I said. He grinned and asked, "Are you relieved that I can play?"

Keith Johnson

ITG Newsletter Welcomes New Editor

Keith Johnson, Associate Professor of Trumpet at the University of Northern Iowa, has been named Music Review Editor for the *ITG Newsletter*. Keith performs in the Northern Brass Quintet and as principal trumpet in the Waterloo-Cedar Falls Symphony Orchestra. He also performs during the summers as a member of the New Hampshire Music Festival Orchestra. His articles on trumpet performance have appeared in *The Instrumentalist*, the *Getzen Gazette*, the *School Musician*, the *NACWPI Journal*, and he is the author of *The Art of Trumpet Playing*, recently published by The Iowa State University Press.

International Trumpet Guild Newsletter, October 1981.
Courtesy of International Trumpet Guild Journal.

Richland School District One

presents

1982 Honor Bands

in concert

Senior Band

James K. Copenhaver, Conductor
Janis S. Cooper, Assistant Conductor
Keith Johnson, Trumpet Soloist

Junior Band

Andy Gowan, Conductor
Robert F. Hare, Assistant Conductor

Clinic Band

Claude Greever, Conductor
L. Anne Farr, Assistant Conductor

March 13, 1982
7:30 P.M.
Dreher Auditorium

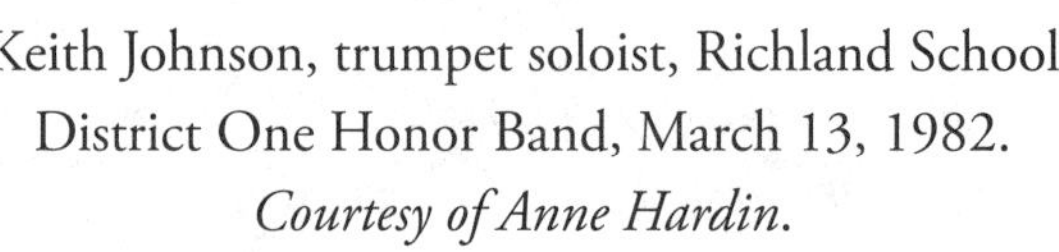

Keith Johnson, trumpet soloist, Richland School
District One Honor Band, March 13, 1982.
Courtesy of Anne Hardin.

Keith's affinity for The Far Side cartoons to brighten people's days didn't surprise me. I know, because a few weeks after we met in Boulder a small package showed up in the ITG postbox. It was from Keith—a classic Far Side coffee mug—the one showing a young student, head down, pushing on the school door for all he's worth. The building is the Midvale School for the Gifted, and the sign on the door says, "Pull." It's been my daily coffee mug for forty years.

Friendship beyond words to express.[40]

Another close friendship that had its beginnings at an ITG conference was that with Brian Shook, chair of the music department at Lamar University:

The night I met Keith Johnson turned out to be the third best meal of my life (only to be surpassed by a honeymoon dinner and a wedding anniversary meal). This was in 2011 just after my biography of William Vacchiano was published. For the previous three years I had been working feverishly on the manuscript along with my editor, and we had been planning to celebrate the culmination of our efforts at the International Trumpet Guild Conference that year in Minneapolis, Minnesota.

What does a dinner with Keith Johnson and a biography of William Vacchiano have in common? The answer is Anne Hardin. I remember her telling me she was good friends with Keith—they were both on the ITG Board—and she would try to line up the dinner so he could celebrate with us at Ruth's Chris Steak House—I was beyond excited! Despite my nervousness, the three of us got along swimmingly and after about five minutes it seemed like we had all been lifelong friends. While the meal was delicious, the conversation and camaraderie were the main course. We must have been there for at least three-and-a-half hours before closing the place down (like any "respectable" trumpet player gathering).

What struck me the most was his ease of character and his genuine spirit—this set him apart from so many, but also was simultaneously magnetic. He was not just a trumpet guru, musical genius, or a preeminent pedagogue (yes, he was all of those things!); he was a caring person who cared about people. He lived this every day not just by what he said, but by how he lived his life—it was in his DNA. The "job" was never done because relationships were the central element of everything he did. Relationships reverberate longer than any applause and they extend beyond the teaching studio—they are eternal.

I was privileged to witness just one such example of this kind of relationship in Keith's life when he and Cecil invited my wife and me to stay with them for a weekend a few years after the dinner in Minneapolis. One of the items on our weekend agenda was to visit was Keith's former teacher and predecessor at UNT, the great John Haynie. Sitting in Mr. Haynie's house with Keith (along with Marilyn, Cecile, and my wife) was about as surreal as it can get. I distinctly remember leaving the Haynie's and getting into the Johnson's car when a wave of emotions came over me. In that instant, everything came into sharp focus. My research on Mr. Vacchiano was still very fresh in my mind and I was acutely aware of the profound influence a teacher can have on a student, but to share an hour with these two men whose lives had so been so indelibly intertwined—and the respect and gratitude Keith had for Mr. Haynie even decades later—brought me to tears.

While I was never a trumpet student of Keith's, I was in some way a life student of his. The lesson here was one of compassion, admiration, and respect. Regardless of who he had become and the many accomplishments he achieved, Keith always remembered those who came before him and invested their lives in him. Keith, in turn, did the same. He did not just impart wisdom, he changed you in a special way that only he could.[41]

In addition to his busy performance schedule, Johnson devoted himself to his trumpet studio and received recognition for his teaching. In 1996, he became the first brass faculty member to be awarded the title of Regents Professor at UNT. In 2011, Johnson was named a University Distinguished Teaching Professor. He also received the UNT College of Music Honor Alumni award in 2016.

In the mid-1990s, Johnson began assisting with the Genesis Foundation's program for collecting instruments to assist in the rebuilding of music education within South Africa. In May 1995, Michael Blake, principal trumpet of the Cape Town Symphony Orchestra and Sean Kierman of University of Cape Town organized a tour in which Johnson presented sixteen clinics in ten days. For the next several years, Johnson returned to South Africa for recitals and clinics and became a member of the Board of Directors of the Genesis Foundation.

One of Johnson's students, Annette Hammett Talley, was inspired by his descriptions of the rebirth of music education in South Africa: "Mr. Johnson's stories of the children, their love for music, and his enjoyment of teaching there, planted a seed in my heart to follow that lead. Because of his experiences I dreamed of going to Africa to teach music. Soon after graduating from UNT, I spent a semester teaching band, choir, and elementary music at the African Bible College in Lilongwe, Malawi. I still have wonderful relationships with the people there almost twenty years later, and I have Mr. Johnson to thank for that."[42]

In 2013, Johnson received a Distinguished Service Award from the New Hampshire Music Festival for fifty years of service as co-principal trumpet of the festival orchestra. He continued to perform in the summer festival until 2017.

Johnson's first book, *The Art of Trumpet Playing*, which was published in1981, brought him national and international recognition. Although it is written as a guide for trumpet players, this text has become popular among players of other brass instruments. This ground breaking book examined the psychology of learning as applied to music, and it emphasized clearly imagining the sound one wants to achieve through directed listening, thus bypassing the action-oriented directions of the conscious mind. Johnson made a persuasive case for changing from the usual physical analysis method of playing to a more artistic approach in which the desired musical product directs the subconscious mind.

His second book, *Brass Performance and Pedagogy*, published in 2002, serves as a guide for those who teach brass instruments. It includes Johnson's philosophy of teaching and covers most of the topics addressed in his first book from a more general perspective that can be applied in teaching all brass instruments.

Both pedagogy books are widely used in colleges and conservatories. He also wrote two method books, *Progressive Studies for the High Register* (Gore Publications) and *Baroque Trumpet Method* (unpublished). Additionally, he authored more than thirty articles that greatly influenced generations of brass players and teachers.

"Mr. Johnson has distilled for us the essence of a deep study of the psychology of learning and the experience of years of performing and teaching. *The Art of Trumpet Playing* is rich and compact, with nothing superfluous. Virtually every page contains passages worth underlining: the kind that one likes to write on a card and put on the wall of the practice room, or pencil in at the top of the etude of the day."
Stephen Chenette, ITG Newsletter, February 1982.
Courtesy of Harold Gore Publishing Co.

"The book opens with a short, although thoroughly concise, text that summarizes those feelings all teachers stress concerning high register development. Johnson writes that in playing in the upper register students should emphasize a singing quality, with stress on musicality—not just hitting high notes, and place emphasis on rest during the practice session."
Thomas Erdmann, ITG Journal Music Reviews, December 1991.
Courtesy of Harold Gore Publishing Co.

"Johnson is gifted at describing aural and other abstract concepts through words. The text is readable and succinct. This book will be extremely valuable to non-brass students in music education methods classes, professional brass teachers, and players at all levels. It is a book we all should own and keep in our trumpet cases."
Karl Sievers, ITG Journal Book Reviews, June 2003.
Courtesy of International Trumpet Guild Journal.

Renaissance Man

Keith Johnson was a man of many interests whose knowledge extended far beyond the field of music. He is remembered as a great conversationalist who enjoyed expounding on history, art, philosophy, and politics. Johnson was also a connoisseur of food, wine, and single malt Scotch, and many of his memorable conversations took place around a table—in historic Dallas cafes, iconic seafood spots, and epicurean buffets, as well as campus eateries.

While at UNT, Marc Reed was a student who enjoyed lunches with Johnson:

It took me about three semesters to learn this, but I always tried to schedule my weekly lesson with Keith at 11 AM on Tuesdays. Why? Because Keith always ate lunch near campus over his lunch hour on Tuesdays and would often invite whatever student he had just finished teaching. For probably six of the nine semesters that I was fortunate to study with KJ, I ate lunch with him on Tuesday at noon almost every week. We talked about all sorts of things and rarely was it trumpet or music. In fact, if I wanted to talk shop, I would have to bring it up and he would usually very kindly answer my question, then change the subject back to wine, food, coffee, Blue Bell ice cream, or the girl I happened to be dating at the time. Keith also never, ever let me pay. When the check would come, he would grab it and tell me that I couldn't afford to pay because I was a poor college student. He'd then say, "One day when you are teaching, you can repay me by taking your own students to lunch." To this day, if I am ever in a situation where I can buy a meal, coffee, or a drink for one of my students, I always pick up the check. It's my little homage to Keith.[43]

When Starbucks opened a store on University Drive in Denton, it became Johnson's second office. He retired a little too soon, as his favorite coffee shop is now on campus. Jason Dovel recalled: "Keith loved Starbucks and went there every day, I believe. Upon my successful dissertation defense, I handed Keith a thank-you card with a personal note, as well as a $100 Starbucks gift card inside. He opened the envelope, saw the card, and exclaimed, 'Ha, this will last me about one week!'"[44]

In addition to his appreciation for fine food and drink, Johnson also loved books. He always enjoyed discussing his current read with students, which could be anything from C. S. Lewis to Kierkegaard to his favorite "trashy British mysteries." He was a committed Anglophile, and the Tudor monarchy, Anglican architecture, and the Church of England were his special interests. Johnson had rooms full of books at home, and when the shelves became too crowded, he would bring them to the Recycled Books store on the Denton Square and invariably take home several more. This continued until a student worker pointed out that he was buying back his own books!

Keith Johnson in his "neighborhood," Studio 272.
Courtesy of Cecile Johnson.

Mr. Johnson's Neighborhood

During my years at North Texas, Johnson always had a Far Side calendar with tear-off cartoons. He would post one on his bulletin board each day, and people from every corner of the College of Music would find a reason to go to the north end of the complex and read the newest comic page at Studio 272. Things could feel rather dark in other areas of the campus, but his hall was known as "Mr. Johnson's Neighborhood." An atmosphere of friendliness and support always radiated from the man who seemed to thumb his nose at much of the red tape and endless forms that characterize a large institution. His concern was always for the students.

One afternoon I dropped by his office for advice on possible dissertation topics and my upcoming recital. He was just leaving, but he set his gym bag down and gave me his full attention. The conversation expanded to include resumes, cover letters, and my goals—all the pressing concerns of a graduate music student. As always, he was generous with encouragement and helpful advice and caught me up on the latest departmental gossip. When our conversation drew to a close, he traded his gym bag for his trumpet case. I was horrified to realize I had been there over an hour and had talked away his workout time. As he put his paperwork into his briefcase, I saw his "We Give a Damn!" button pinned to the interior, and thought to myself, "Yes, he really does!"

Johnson is remembered by his students as the quintessential college professor, often attired in a tweed jacket and cap, but he is even more appreciated for his dedication to teaching. Kurt Gorman recalls:

Keith was the consummate professor, to the point of parody, occasionally sporting one of his "economics professor" bow ties as he referred to them, or with his affinity for fine wine, cuisine, single malt Scotch, and the Mercedes he drove.

Keith's persona was strong enough that he hasn't needed to be present for most of my lessons. Whenever I pick up a trumpet, I hear in my mind's ear some thoughtful comment that he may or may not have actually said to me. It is not dogmatic or judgmental—it is encouraging and patient and wise. The essence of it is cultivating or healing.

It seems strange now, but I somehow remember my first advising session with Keith. It fell on his fifty-second birthday in August 1994, during which he told me he was planning a fifty-two-mile bike ride later that day in commemoration. I told him I would be happy to join him for about the first two miles, but my bike had been stolen on the South Side of Chicago the year before. That produced a sideways glance and a chuckle. The session ended with his mentioning his financial planner and postulating that he'd never be able to retire. It later became pretty clear to me that he'd probably continue to work forever, and it would not be a remunerative decision.[45]

Two traits that stood out in Johnson's teaching were his warm disposition and his talent for simplifying the challenges of the instrument by using the music itself to get the best responses. Jason Dovel described that simplicity:

Keith Johnson was world-renowned for a pedagogy that was robust, specific, clear, and well-thought-out. But for me, it was never what he said, but *how* he said it. He was the wise grandfather with the gentle temperament of a seasoned teacher; he had an uncanny ability to describe the most complicated pedagogical concepts in such simple terms. And what's more, as he delivered his remarks, his calm demeanor always put you at ease.

After I had moved from Texas to Oklahoma for my first university appointment, I came down for what turned out to be my final lesson before my last DMA recital. I was playing a difficult French piece rather poorly; in particular I was having trouble producing a good sound and being accurate. Keith calmly walked up to me, put his hand on my shoulder, and simply said, "Jason, think of your tongue being a bit lower in your mouth." It was like magic. Instantly, my response was better, my sound was fuller, and my accuracy improved. I will never forget that moment, and how such a simple instruction yielded such incredible results.[46]

James Wood also experienced Johnson's ability to reduce the complexities of the instrument by focusing on the musical result desired:

When I started at UNT, the knowledge I brought from my previous teachers—Steve Jones, Armando Ghitalla, Charles Schlueter, and Vince Cichowicz—all competed for dominance in my head. I hadn't yet been able to combine them into what would eventually become my own unique sound and approach to trumpet playing. Keith was able to help me narrow my focus, accept what I inherently knew, and just deliver the music, using the trumpet as a vessel. Keith honed the concept I learned from Vincent Cichowicz, that inhalation should take on the same character of exhalation, with no distinction between. No "hitch" or hesitation at the top of the inhale, just a continuous breath. He summarized this with his simple phrase, "Ah- Tu." That concept alone, once finally mastered, propelled my playing into an entirely new phase.

Something else that helped immensely during my first year at UNT was sitting next to Rob Murray, another Keith Johnson DMA student. The adage, "If you want to improve, sit next to someone better than you," was never truer than when I sat next to Rob in the Wind Symphony. I saw all Keith's teachings exemplified in him, and was flabbergasted when, without seeming to move a muscle, Rob took a breath, and pure golden sound emanated from his bell. Keith's and Rob's approach was the Tai Chi of trumpet playing, as opposed to a more aggressive approach found in other studios.

The other concept that stands out is this: Find a musical solution to a technical problem. I have always been a more musical player than a technical one, excelling at lyrical, soaring melodies, and struggling at extreme technical passages. Keith taught me that rather than strug-gling against the technical challenges of a piece, once the hours of slow practice were done, to think about the inherent music within the phrase. Where is the phrase coming from? Where is it going? This concept, combined with his axiom, "Play every note as if it's your last," made me realize that I shouldn't treat those intense technical passages as a gauntlet to survive, but as a challenge to embrace. Suddenly, Tomasi wasn't so daunting.[47]

The trumpet students appreciated the positive environment in the studio and the results they were experiencing. Eric Swisher expressed his curiosity about how Johnson was helping him to improve:

My first several lessons with Keith were astonishing. I came into each lesson with a long list of issues that needed attention. Sometimes the list was in my head, other times I wrote it down (which always amused him). But each time I entered his office frustrated, I left playing much better. Everything in between was a blur. My trumpet issues had been resolved, but I didn't know how. I was baffled.

For the benefit of my students, I wanted to figure out how he was doing this. How was he "fixing" my playing without my direct knowledge? I started to pay attention to his pedagogy. Not surprisingly, he demanded excellent fundamentals: a good breath, a good sound, as well as clear phrasing. However, the difference was how he talked about it. He taught proper technique, but did it through musicianship. There was very little talk about parts and functions of the body. In so doing, he was able to bypass the part of my brain that was getting in the way. He kept me thinking about music which allowed my body to do its job without mental interference. This was only possible because of the trust I had in him as a trumpet teacher and more importantly, as a friend.[48]

How did he do that? I believe the answer to that is largely about his approach to the people he was teaching, whether in private lessons, studio and masterclasses, or other settings. The music making was intense, but the atmosphere was relaxed, enjoyable, and encouraging. Johnson often quoted Cichowicz, saying: "Every student has a measure that he can play as well as Maurice André. It's the teacher's job to find that measure and build on it."

Johnson raised this idea to an art form. In my first semester of lessons as a graduate student, I remember thinking that I had been taking trumpet lessons since high school, and I couldn't remember anyone shouting "Wonderful!" after a good phrase, or even a good breath. He always found something he could build on.

Other students, like Calvin Hofer, experienced this approach from a different angle: "I asked Mr. Johnson to edit a review I was working on for the ITG Journal. He read it, and circled one sentence and said, 'That's a good sentence.' He then began making other suggestions to the article. That too, was a wonderful learning moment from the master!"[49]

Ward Yager shared an example of Johnson's commitment to helping students develop confidence and maintain their perspective in the competitive atmosphere of the largest music school in the nation:

In my second semester at UNT, I walked into a lesson with a lot of frustration and sadness. I had been having a hard time, struggling with my playing and feeling like I wasn't going to make it. Keith quickly realized I wasn't doing well, and he suggested we have one of his "coffee" lessons. So, we walked to the UNT Student Union and he bought me coffee.

After some small talk, he asked what was wrong. I admitted that I didn't feel at the level of my fellow students, and that I had too many issues to overcome. My confidence was definitely at a low. I wish I remember his exact words but basically, he said how ridiculous my comments were. He explained the worst thing I could do was compare individual aspects of trumpet playing to the entire studio of a hundred and twenty trumpet majors. His reason was that for every facet of sound, technique, and musicianship, there were at least five (if not more) people at UNT for whom that was their specialty. And it was virtually impossible for any one person to compare him or herself to such a large studio!

Simply put: He told me to be the best I could be, using my colleagues' abilities and knowledge as great resources to inspire me. This perspective and his kind words helped change my outlook. It's a lesson I'll never forget.[50]

David Spencer was one of many who noted Johnson's warmth and generosity with his time:

I remember quite vividly the evening we met. It was at the Texas Music Educators Conference in San Antonio, Texas. My dear friend Scott Whitfield had suggested we go to a reception hosted by the College of Music. I was planning to audition for graduate school in a few months and Scott had mentioned that Keith might be a good teacher for me. So, off we went.

We soon found ourselves with the requisite plastic cups of wine in hand and as luck would have it, Keith was "enjoying" the same. I include this as a bit of irony given so many who knew how much Keith enjoyed tasting and talking about wine!

While I had my best professional face on, I have to say in retrospect, Mr. Johnson was just his usual welcoming self that we all came to know: genuine, honest, and encouraging. He joked that if I came in the fall, I would be the first graduate student he recruited at UNT, "and over a plastic cup of wine, no less." We discussed my plans and he suggested I come up and see him that next weekend for a lesson. I was teaching public school in the Rio Grande Valley but could fly up to Dallas that weekend.

While we had dozens of great lessons and pedagogical discussions over the course of our time together, those first lessons in the winter of 1987 were so meaningful to my future. It was not only the content and the concepts he was teaching me, but more important, it was the sacrifice of making time for me on a Saturday or Sunday when he really didn't need to. That made a profound statement to me and has shaped my outlook as a college teacher. I am always reminded of his kindness whenever I receive an email or a call or a request from a student. I try my best to pass on that goodwill that Keith so generously showed.[51]

Etienne Stoupy was another who experienced Johnson's helpfulness while at UNT:

I remember my first trumpet lesson with Keith Johnson. I was very nervous and worried about making a good first impression as a potential student. I had only moved to the United States from France a couple of years prior to our meeting. Keith talked about French wine and tried to make me feel at home, and I immediately thought to myself, "I like this guy." We spent most of the lesson working on the "perfect breath" and by the time we got into the Chaynes trumpet concerto, I felt more at ease and got the best sound I could have on that day.

My first year at UNT was financially rough. Being from France with no family living in the United States, I had to pay out-of-state tuition, but Keith came up with a scholarship for me that would reduce my tuition. He didn't have to do that, but he did it because it was the right thing to do. I know there are probably many other stories just like mine that demonstrate his generosity as a teacher and human.[52]

Many of Johnson's students and colleagues mention the example he set as a role model, always courteous and professional. This too, was something he expected from all of his students. One of his doctoral students, Raquel Samayoa, who now teaches trumpet at UNT, related this story:

> Keith had a way of not allowing students to bring any sense of arrogance to lessons or with interactions among students in the studio. I had an unfortunate incident with some of my peers in a brass quintet. He heard about what happened and asked me to meet with him. He let me know in no uncertain terms that arrogant behavior would not be tolerated in his studio and also warned me of this behavior in a professional setting. Keith, a consummate professional, helped me reach my potential as a trumpet player while also teaching me how to become a better person. These life lessons helped me in my career and in relationships with future colleagues.[53]

Approach to Teaching

Johnson alluded to the influence of Vincent Cichowicz in his own teaching many times in lessons and classes. He described Cichowicz as a gentleman who was persuasive by inner conviction, a teacher who was hardly ever negative. Many of Keith Johnson's students quoted throughout this book mention the same qualities in Johnson's teaching.

In Trevor Duell's interview, Johnson spoke about his regard for Vincent Cichowicz: "There were so many wonderful things about his teaching, but the thing that was most wonderful was when I left my lesson with him, I felt I was at the center of his world. I can't imagine I make that same impression with my students, at least to that degree, but if I could end up doing that, I would be very pleased. That's what he did for me. I felt I was the main concern of his life for that hour. He was an extraordinary force."[54]

As a teacher, Johnson followed in the Cichowicz tradition: he gave completely of himself and was totally involved with what his students were doing. He often said, "You teach by what you are, even more than what you say." He was devoted to his students and had a real attachment and commitment to each of us. He was passionate about playing, teaching, and getting these ideas across to the next generation.

In his pedagogy classes and lessons, Johnson repeatedly emphasized, "You are not teaching the trumpet, you are teaching the student!" Johnson also stressed the importance of a positive environment:

> Present what you're trying to get across in the most positive way. Tell your student what was really good about a passage. You might mention something if the student has overlooked it, but draw attention to the good things, the beauty. Remember why you play the trumpet in the first place. That's why we are still playing now.
>
> Assume that the student wants to learn to play. Give him credit; in the long run it will show up. The student should leave the room in a positive mood unless he's not doing any work—then it's all right to cut him off at the knees.[55]

Johnson was well aware of the difficulties faced by serious students, including those in his own studio: "Don't forget that the student has trouble distinguishing between the value of himself as an individual and as a player. If he leaves depressed, ask yourself how you're teaching him. The student is often under more self-imposed tension than the teacher realizes. It is very easy to trigger a bad response. The student is not as detached as you are. For a serious student, his lesson is a very special event once a week. Get him to view it as a comfortable, secure performing experience."[56]

At the end of his teaching career, Johnson spoke about the principles governing his teaching:

> I have always tried to teach musicians that play the trumpet as opposed to training trumpet players. I also want to make sure that no student leaves thinking they know everything. That's not to suggest I think they aren't smart, but I want them to always be open and questioning—in a positive way. Be open to new ideas and thoughts because everything changes. Change is the one constant. I think if we don't change, we atrophy. Every year you ought to be a little smarter, a little more musical, a little more enthusiastic. I hope all my students will remain curious.
>
> It's important to take care of yourself physically and mentally too. You do that by reading books, listening to new recordings. Listen way beyond the boundaries of your performance focus. Not just trumpet recordings but string quartets, opera, piano music. Be an informed

musician, not just a trumpet player. I want my students to keep grow-ing! I think that's important for all of us. Strive to be an interested and interesting musician. Keep moving! That's the main thing. Moving targets are harder to hit.[57]

Johnson retired from UNT after the spring semester of 2014. True to form, he continued on an adjunct basis the following year to teach out his grad-uate students. He wrote a short statement on "Why I Teach" in the *North Texan*: "I had a choice of performing or teaching. I chose teaching—the right choice—and am surrounded by colleagues who are gifted, devoted to teaching, performing, and to their students. Every day, I learn new things. I hear the progress my students are making and share their achievements. After almost fifty years, I go to work each day with gratitude and anticipa-tion. What a great journey it has been."[58]

Studio Stories

I was one of Keith Johnson's first students at UNT, as a senior in his first year there (1986). Something happened shortly before graduation and now that I am a professor myself, I cannot help but wonder if it was a strange situation for him.

I was in Tyler playing with the East Texas Symphony and checked my messages on my home phone in Denton. There was a message from the personnel manager of the Dallas Symphony saying to call him back right away, they needed another trumpet player for the next morning's rehearsal and the three concerts that weekend. Of course, I was excited and said, "Yes."

I then realized I did not own a set of tails, so in my excitement of telling Keith about the opportunity, I asked if I could borrow his since we were the same height. He graciously said, "Of course," and congratulated me on getting the call.

It wasn't until a few years later that I realized it may have been somewhat disappointing to him not getting the call himself as the new professional in town, before a student did. The fact was, I had been studying with DSO Principal Rick Giangiulio in the summers, so he thought of me, and Keith was still very new in town. In any case, I knew he was happy for me and that meant a lot.

Steve Leisring
University of Kansas[59]

During the first year of my master's degree, I always used to bring my mini-disc recorder to my lessons and record them. I still have the first six or seven lessons I ever took with him and they are great. About mid-term I sensed that Keith would occasionally hold back when he was about to delve into one of his legendary stories. So, the next lesson, I didn't bring my recorder. Keith told me some wonderfully entertaining and educational stories. I *never brought my recorder with me to my lesson after. A few years later, during my DMA studies with him, I finally got the nerve to ask him about this. He confessed and said, "I'm not going to live forever, Marc. I'll have no control over who you play those tapes to after I'm dead." Then he laughed like hell.*

Marc Reed
University of Akron[60]

I still chuckle when I remember he would whisper when saying something subversive, "Just in case John Ashcroft is listening." Or how he taught me to sign his name so that he wouldn't have to "sign so many silly forms." I also remember his favorite St. Augustine quote "Love God, and do what you will," which he used when he wanted to encourage me to do what was right and not worry about some particularly silly rule.

Eric Swisher
Murray State University[61]

Prior to coming to the University of North Texas, I was a student of George Novak at Bowling Green State University. During my last day in Bowling Green, Mr. Novak said to me, "Once you're at UNT, let me know how it's going and what it's like studying with Keith Johnson." After two or three weeks at UNT, I remembered Mr. Novak's request and sat down with the intention of sending him the email report he had requested.

I wrote a detailed, lengthy email discussing my time at UNT, and mentioned that I thought lessons were going well, and that Keith Johnson seemed to be pleased with my work. I remember specifically writing about the "rare repertoire" Mr. Novak had given me to take to my first lessons and how I thought Keith really enjoyed hearing this unfamiliar music.

However, I made one critical mistake. This email was about *Keith Johnson. Rather than send that email to George Novak, I accidently sent that email* to *Keith Johnson!! Thankfully it was all positive email saying nothing but upbeat things about my lessons with Keith. Upon receiving that email Keith immediately responded with the following: "I am pleased that you are pleased that I am pleased."*

Jason Dovel

University of Kentucky[62]

Upon my arrival to begin my DMA at North Texas, Keith requested to meet for our initial lesson. Being from the Pacific Northwest, I was accustomed to rain, but not the torrential "frog stranglers" that pound Texas from time to time. Anyway, I parked my truck about 6 blocks away and began the walk towards the music building ... just as it started to rain. No—I did not have an umbrella! About ten steps later, the deluge ensued. I didn't want to miss my very first lesson- so I ran the rest of the way. Needless to say, I was totally drenched by the time I arrived at Keith's air-conditioned office.

Keith looked at me oddly and said, "Are you sure you want to play?" I replied, "I'm already here, so yes—let's play." About twenty minutes in, I was cold and shaking uncontrollably, not a best first impression! Anyway, I finally asked Keith if I could take off my shirt because I figured I would be warmer without it. He replied "Ummm ... I suppose so" but was clearly uncomfortable with the proceeding. So I removed my shirt and we finished the lesson. When done, I stood up to leave and there was literally a puddle of water on his floor! I thanked him for his time and his only words were, "Get an umbrella!" We laughed many times about my first lesson ... a story I share with all my students in North Carolina! A great friend and mentor.

Larry Wells

Methodist University[63]

Sometime during my second year at North Texas, I was packing up at the end of a lesson while enjoying the usual banter with Keith talking about life, music, and nothing special. On this particular day, he was lamenting the fact that the Dean had authorized some remodeling of the administrative suite near the music office. In vintage Johnson style, he was expressing his concern over money devoted to create a fancy meeting place, while the rest of the school settled for the same furniture they had been using for years. He asked, "Have you seen what's going on up there?" Then, while shaking his head and gesturing to the old furniture in his office, he said, "And this is what the rest of us get." I recall that he seemed particularly upset about the upscale office chairs that could be easily seen through the new plate glass windows in the refurbished meeting area. I remember thinking to myself, "Wow, he's really upset about this whole chair thing."

Now, there are few things in life I have experienced that evoke the same joy as a well-delivered rant by Keith: so clear, so informed, so passionate. I have encountered few people with the same ability to articulate frustration in such a concise, yet elegant way. Come to think of it, his ability to articulate anything was next level. The same skill he possessed in delivering advanced pedagogical concepts with brilliant clarity could also be used to put a fine point on his displeasure with someone or something in the most eloquent and efficient manner. It was a gift. A gift that brought me great joy. And to be honest, the more "passionate" he was, the more amusing I found it. And he knew it. It was, simply put, his superpower.

The next day when I arrived on campus, I learned from several people that Keith was looking for me. I made my way to his office and knocked on the door. Instead of just yelling, "Come in!" as he usually did, he opened the door, stuck his head out, looked both ways as if to see whether I had been followed, and said, "Get in here!" At this juncture, he pointed across the room and said, "What have you done?!" He was pointing, of course, at two of the new luxury leather chairs that, until the evening before, had been located in the new administrative suite outside the Dean's office. I responded by making some comment about how nice the chairs were. "Don't give me that. How did they get here?!"

Now, not much surprised Keith. But in that moment, he was truly flabbergasted. The best part was his trying to do the right thing, get to the bottom of it, and scold me in some way for moving university property. But he just couldn't keep a straight face. That wry smile was breaking through the entire time. I held my ground. After all, I wanted to protect him. He could never tell what he didn't really know. He was so happy and that made me happy.

Until now, I have maintained my innocence in this great mystery. Keith told the story many times over the years (like every time we were together and there was someone to listen). In fact, one of my students has an audio recording of his sharing details of the now-infamous event over dinner one evening when Keith came to visit my school. He loved telling that story and I loved hearing it. His masterful ability to recount the events of "The Great Chair Caper" is a memory I will cherish for the rest of my life.

By the way, he did love those chairs. And so he kept them, of course.

Bill Stowman
Messiah University[64]

During the fall of my last year as a DMA student, UNT was making some equipment improvements. The Murchison Performing Arts Center bought new Wenger chairs, padded with nice blue fabric. In one lesson, Keith asked me if I'd seen the new chairs, and I said I had. With a sheepish grin, he told me that he hated the old student chairs he'd been using in his office and would love a couple like the ones that had just been bought. He then went on a long diatribe about how faculty can't buy things that they should rightfully have for their offices.

The next day after Wind Symphony rehearsal, I grabbed two new stage chairs, walked out of the building in broad daylight, and placed them in Keith's studio, adorned with huge red bows. When I came in for my next lesson, he sat for a few moments, ran his hand down the side of his chair, and said, "Thank you!" with one of the biggest grins I'd ever seen.

A few months after I'd swiped the chairs, UNT bought a supply of bright "Mean Green" music stands. Keith said the Dean was angry that students kept stealing the black music stands for gigs and not returning them. Buying green stands was the COM's answer. Keith then asked me point blank, "Could you get me a green stand for my office? It would look great with my new chairs."

Marc Reed
University of Akron[65]

Keith Johnson and William Stowman at the International
Trumpet Guild Conference in 2009.
Courtesy of William Stowman.

On the Road

My most memorable gig with Keith Johnson was playing Baroque trumpet with the Orchestra of New Spain. We flew to Albuquerque the day after Christmas and had a late afternoon dress rehearsal in a cold, dark church. He was playing a British four-hole-model trumpet, which another instrument maker has famously described as "all curtain rods and doorknobs, but the bloody things work!" As the rehearsal proceeded, we heard a buzzing from his instrument, which became progressively more noticeable, until finally the bloody thing didn't work at all.

This model is sold as an unassembled jumble of metal yards, bits, and crooks, to allow the instrument to be assembled in any of several different keys. Most players use a guide sheet to ensure correct assembly for each key. I was grateful for my relatively simple three-piece Swiss instrument.

Keith began testing each length of tubing for leaks by plugging one end with his finger and blowing through the other. He enlisted my help for the main yards, which are nearly three feet long. Because we were performing music in two keys, there were many pieces of tubing to check, and soon we both had a lapful of "curtain rods." Meanwhile, the conductor was glaring at us for not playing.

After several minutes, Johnson discovered that a piece of solder around a fingerhole had worked loose, causing the buzzing noise. We had no metalworking equipment, of course, and no time to find a shop. I began asking other musicians if they had any gum, when Keith said, "Go get one of those candles!" With a blob of wax and a "Hail Mary" he was ready to go, and the concert went very well. I believe we both left some money in the candle box.

Other students and colleagues have shared their favorite gig stories, as well, such as this one from Keith Benjamin of the University of Missouri-Kansas City Conservatory:

Many years ago, Keith and I were playing The Nutcracker with the Waterloo-Cedar Falls Symphony. The orchestra was on the floor right in front of the stage because there was no pit. During the performances, I was sitting literally knee to knee with an audience member in the front row, with Keith directly to my right. For some reason, he gave the stupid kid—me—the "toy trumpet" part and suggested I play it up an octave on muted piccolo trumpet … or maybe that was my stupid kid idea.

At the first performance I wailed away on this solo and blacked out. The last thing I saw was the conductor, Joe Giunta, looking rather quizzically my way. I regained consciousness a few seconds later, more than half in the lap of the poor woman sitting in the audience to my left, sans horn. Keith had grabbed it and let me fall over. I looked at him in confusion, and he said, sotto voce, "I thought I'd better save the more important bit."[66]

David Spencer of the University of Memphis enjoyed several foreign trips with Johnson and has recalled some highlights:

Keith and I made our first international trip together in 1997 when he invited me to be part of a trumpet delegation from UNT to perform the Khachaturian Third Symphony with the Orquesta Sinfonica de Mineria in Mexico City. He and I also stayed an extra week to play the off-stage parts for the Verdi Requiem. By this time, Keith and I had established a robust portfolio of memorable dining experiences in the U.S. This would give us two weeks of uninterrupted, back-to-back opportunities to eat and drink our way through the largest city in the Western Hemisphere, including the only outpost of Mexico City's Alfredo Di Roma of fettuccini fame.

David Spencer and Keith Johnson in Sillico, Italy.
Courtesy of David Spencer.

Keith and I got to spend a lot of time together that second week, talking about careers, life, retirement, and shopping for art. In fact, we both brought back paintings we purchased at the San Angel art market. My acquisition still hangs proudly in remembrance of that trip. I know that Keith's did as well. (It was that yellow one in the den for those of you in the know). Keith and I found out that we both shared a love of contemporary painting. It was also the week that Princess Diana died. I came to understand his love of all things British that week, as well.

In the spring of 2005, Keith and I made a trip to Italy. He had heard of the Baroque trumpet seminar hosted by Paul Thomas, and the featured artist that year was to be Stephen Keavy, from whom Keith had just purchased a trumpet. As a side note, I learned a day or so after we arrived that Keith really wanted to come because he had dropped his bag of trumpet parts to his new Keavy and since they had no markings, was at a complete loss as to what pieces went together!! It got solved, thankfully, and Keith felt like the whole trip was worth it!

In July 2011, I took a two-year leave from my position at Memphis to be the founding director of a new music academy housed at the Escola Americana in Campinas, Brazil, and to serve as International Professor of Brass at the Conservatorio Nacional in Tatui, Brazil. Armed with a. nice budget for guest artists, I invited Keith to come down for a week to work with the students of the Academy (eleven to twenty-year-olds) and at the University of Campinas School for the Arts.

Keith was a hit, of course, and it was the first time I had seen how consummate a teacher he really was. All his former students can attest to how clearly and concisely he communicated his ideas, but to see the same principles in action with beginners and young students was particularly rewarding for me. It was pure Keith. Despite the elementary level of the youngest students at the Academy, Keith was able to relate and teach them as if he had been teaching at that level his entire life. The next day we were at the University working with the trumpet studio led by Dr. Paulo Ronqui. Keith was his usual best. What was more remarkable and memorable to me, however, was the seamlessness of Keith's teaching. I always knew, from a personal perspective, that he possessed great skills as a teacher, but I realized something different during his time in Brazil. He has always stated that teaching is an art but I witnessed it first- hand during our time there. It didn't matter who or at what level Keith was teaching, he was as comfortable and effective with the doctoral students as he was with an eleven-year-old all within a span of twenty-four hours!

In retrospect, I was so lucky to have the uninterrupted time with Keith. His mentorship outside the lessons was some of the most formative and important times we spent with him and those that resonate most. Keith taught us so much about pedagogy and music but mostly he was concerned that we always should be good, interesting people. I hope we never forget that even on our worst day.[67]

Etianne Stoupy of the Acadiana Symphony Orchestra reflects, "I have wonderful memories of driving with Keith to our gig in Dallas every year at Christmas. Instead of listening to music, we would talk and laugh about how he had cheated on his diet. He would pick a great restaurant to eat before the gig. Rather than choosing a healthy option, he would get the steak and say, 'Don't tell Cecile!'"[68]

As John Cord of Luther College recounts:

One of my most treasured memories was playing a simple church job in Fort Worth with Keith sometime around 2010. He was near retirement at that point, but was playing first trumpet and leading a quartet of two trumpets and two trombones through a thicket of repeat signs, stanzas, interludes, hand signal cues, etc. Keith never missed a single detail while playing the challenging first trumpet parts with such firmness—it was a real joy to observe such professionalism. We played jobs together often, and this was always the case. I learned as much from watching him perform as I did from his lessons and masterclasses.[69]

Changing of the Guard

In 2015, Jason Bergman was hired to succeed Johnson in the UNT Trumpet Department. Bergman describes his tenure there:

Keith Johnson was present at my audition recital the day I interviewed at UNT. He was tremendously gracious and kind to me. Our interaction that day started a cherished friendship, and my family became close to Keith and Cecile.

I enjoyed attending student recitals with Keith. He often shared special stories with me about the past at UNT. I turned to him for advice and counsel, and he was always generous with both, but encouraged me to follow my instincts, because he had complete faith in me.

While I enjoyed my time with Keith and Cecile in Denton, I fondly remember the first time we met. My first meeting happened when I was in high school. I am originally from the Dallas/Ft. Worth area, and I was hired for an Easter service at a church in the metroplex. As is typical, it was a brass quintet service. However, to my great surprise, when I showed up for the rehearsal, Keith Johnson was the other trumpet player! He had his Monette trumpet and was dressed in a very nice suit. I'm sure he was shocked and disappointed that the other trumpet player was a high school kid and not a top-level professional. I was surprised to see him, as well, and immediately became nervous. Here I was playing with a legend and I didn't want to disappoint him. In true Keith Johnson fashion, he was so kind and welcoming. He didn't let me see any disappointment, and much like he later did when I got to UNT, he showed faith in me and encouraged me to be confident in my abilities. I'll never forget that experience.

Additionally, after winning the position at UNT, I was invited to perform with him at the New Hampshire Music Festival in 2015. Keith and Cecile had been there for over fifty years of summer performances. We were able to spend time talking about the rich history of UNT, getting to know each other better and to talk about the future. The good fortune of spending so much quality time with him that summer is another experience I will cherish.

I was so happy at North Texas. I felt the weight of the past and wanted to live up to the standard that John Haynie, Leonard Candelaria, Keith Johnson, and John Holt had set. I worked hard to connect with alumni, all the previous trumpet teachers, and to help to build the studio for a new generation of success. I was there for three years and really felt as though we were on that trajectory.

I never anticipated that I would leave UNT. I had just received tenure and was excited about the future. That was the point when my alma mater, Brigham Young University, offered me the position and I was able to replace my teacher, David Brown, who had just retired. It was the right move for my family and I wish nothing but the best for the UNT trumpet studio. I deeply value my friendships with Keith and Cecile Johnson, Mrs. Haynie, and Dr. Candelaria. They were always supportive, kind, and generous.[70]

After Bergman's departure, the College of Music conducted another trumpet search, and hired two new teachers to augment the trumpet faculty: Caleb Hudson and Raquel Samayoa. Hudson is a graduate of The Juilliard School and performs with Canadian Brass. Samayoa performs with Seraph Brass and the Lantana Trio and was a student of Keith Johnson's while earning her DMA at North Texas. She brings together the pedagogical ideas of both John Haynie and Keith Johnson in her teaching and pays tribute to them here:

The UNT Trumpet Studio Today

By Raquel Samayoa, University of North Texas

Teaching at the University of North Texas has been the honor of my life. I have a picture of John Haynie and Keith Johnson hanging in my office. I use Haynie's book *How to Play High Notes, Low Notes, and All Those in Between* with my students to teach technique. I also have graduate students read Keith's books, *The Art of Trumpet Playing* and *Brass Performance and Pedagogy*, to assist in their knowledge of brass pedagogy. Both Keith and my undergraduate teacher, David Ritter, studied with John Haynie at UNT, which makes me part of the Haynie lineage.

Keith's pedagogy was based on the Chicago style of playing, and he loved to talk and write about brass pedagogy. He was very adamant about taking a good breath and basing one's playing on what one heard, rather than felt, while playing. This helped my playing and is also what I teach my students.

Keith was very devoted to John Haynie and included Mr. Haynie in the trumpet studio as much as possible. Keith wanted current students to get to know Mr. Haynie. For example, he took me to Mr. Haynie's house one day to meet him and get a lesson. It was a wonderful lesson and we had a great visit. Afterwards, Mr. Haynie came to some of my DMA recitals. He would also give Keith some notes to give to me concerning my playing at the recitals. His comments were very insightful and helpful. Mr. Johnson's admiration for his predecessor had an impact on me. I was similarly respectful to my predecessors at my first and second jobs, which were at Northern Kentucky University and Tennessee Tech University, respectively.

The applied trumpet faculty at UNT includes John Holt, Caleb Hudson, Adam Gordon, and me. We also have two wonderful jazz trumpet professors, Rob Parton and Philip Dizack.

We have good synergy and the studio is full of talented and hardworking students. The number of trumpet students is now capped at ninety-one, and there are four graduate teaching fellows. I am confident that the UNT trumpet studio has a bright future. The trumpet professors are devoted to bringing the best educational experience to their students. Each major professor teaches a studio class, which is open to all students. We also rotate teaching duties of the UNT trumpet departmental, which still occurs in the Recital Hall on Wednesdays at noon.

Students are the beneficiaries of great recitals, concerts, and guest artists. UNT is a wonderful place for trumpet students because of the wide variety of experiences and opportunities. The trumpet studio, one of the largest in the nation, also provides a healthy competitive culture that can benefit students as they prepare for the competitive field of music. UNT is a place full of history and has a legacy of producing great teachers and musicians. The trumpet faculty are devoted to continuing the great trumpet tradition at UNT.

Raquel Samayoa and Keith Johnson.
Courtesy of Raquel Samayoa.

Part Two

Pedagogy

A Keith Johnson Compendium

In Keith Johnson's brass pedagogy course and studio classes, every lecture was a well-crafted exposition of the topic for the day. In addition to discussing approaches for teaching beginning brass students and advanced players, these talks also included his advice to the next generation of performers and educators on coaching themselves and maintaining successful teaching and performing careers.

Several years ago, I presented a paper on pulmonary function for brass players at a trumpet symposium in Cornwall, England. Keith Johnson, always supportive, was sitting on the front row. I began my remarks by saying, "It's hard to talk about breathing without plagiarizing my teacher." Likewise, describing Johnson's pedagogy is a daunting task. His two books and many articles are so eloquently written that, rather than trying to comment on his writings, I decided to collect and organize the pedagogical concepts he developed during six decades of performing and teaching.

In compiling this section, I attempted to retain the conversational style that Johnson used in his UNT classes. I started with my own notes from classes and lessons, which I then augmented with Johnson's notebooks and handwritten outlines for masterclasses and conference presentations.

In addition to the pedagogical topics, these notes describe Johnson's view of music as metaphor, touch on his philosophy of music education, and leave us with an overarching view of what he called "The Art of Teaching."

His longer presentations and class outlines usually began with four topics: the learning process, developing a concept of sound, listening (the most critical musical skill), and breathing (the most important physical skill). Johnson believed these ideas to be the foundation of good brass playing, with all other skills dependent upon these four things. The remaining topics are presented alphabetically for convenient reference.

Basic Concepts: Learning

There are two ways to view the learning process. It can be seen as very simple or very complex, and both views are correct. The simpler, more creative approach is what most performers actually use. The analytical approach requires a detailed understanding of many factors and, while important for teachers, is not necessary in order to play well.

In understanding how people learn, two things are paramount: imitation and empathy. We learn most skills through imitation. However, brass teaching often begins with physical instructions—what to do with lips, fingers, tongue, and so forth—rather than giving the student a clear example of the desired sound. By contrast, using imitation, the student hears a pitch and, through a process of repeated practice, the resulting sound eventually matches what the player has heard. Allowing students to hear the desired sound repeatedly will direct their efforts more efficiently than starting with physical instruction. Over time, this process of imitation will build their aural memory of the characteristic sound of the instrument.

More advanced students also benefit from learning by imitation. Sophisticated concepts of tone quality, styles of articulation, releases, vibrato, musical inflection, and musical styles are best learned by hearing good examples. When learning by imitation, students at all levels should be allowed to make mistakes as a part of the learning process. We don't need to "fix" an embouchure; instead, we must allow for experimenting or trial and error, until the right connection is made between the aural stimulus and the player's performance.

The instructions necessary for producing the sound are inherent in the desired sound. Of course, results won't be perfect the first time, but if allowed to experiment, the student will discover what he needs to do—as long as we don't get in the way.

The single biggest problem in young players today is that they don't know how they should sound. One cannot hope to play well without hearing the best examples. In talking to most students, you will find that, while favorite athletes are well known and followed closely, students don't always make the same connections in music. Therefore, the teacher should provide the students with as much good stimuli as possible by giving them many fine examples for listening. Recordings are good, but teachers should also demonstrate on their own horn, even if playing a different instrument. There are many things in common between good sound produced on trumpet and on clarinet: fullness, smooth and relaxed breath, a good musical line, and so on. Students should be given a good aural image, without concern that brass players might try to sound like a clarinet.

In addition to understanding the role of imitation in learning, it is important to be able to empathize with students. It's difficult to learn a skill that is intrinsically foreign. Anyone, no matter how capable, can feel awkward or embarrassed when learning a new skill. Keep in mind how much a student has to deal with at first. Even older students can stumble over simple techniques or basic sight-reading when starting a new instrument.

A really fine music teacher can significantly help almost any student on almost any instrument. William Kincaid of the Philadelphia Orchestra, for example, sent one of his flute students to study with pianist Rudolph Serkin. We need to teach principles of good playing and good musicianship rather than trying to give our students a "pre-flight check list" of things to think about before or while playing.

When teaching, express ideas in a simple, creative approach. For breathing, find an image that conjures up fullness and relaxation: "Like a string player using the full bow—use frog to tip breathing." "Think of blowing a sailboat away from you." Work on creating good habits by engaging the imagination and relating to a familiar image or action.

For any creative act, it is necessary to understand the task you are trying to accomplish. Many teachers start in the middle—how to play, rather than how it should sound. The entire process should be based on the idea that the music comes first. As an analogy, the player is the plant manager. If a green car is desired, the manager needs a sophisticated idea of the shade of green, but does not occupy himself with what the production line is doing. Presuming good functioning, the player, like the plant manager, should think of the end, not the means.

Question: What do you do with a student who still has a tight sound after trying all of these things? There are three things you can do: continue to do the right things, determine if there is a specific reason rather than systemic tightness, or give up. You won't be able to teach everyone. Some you can't reach; others are unreachable. When you encounter this, they might be ill-suited to the instrument. Also, they might be lacking good musical skills. Not all students will be as dedicated as you are.

In Johnson's experience, more often than not the best first-year college trumpet students were those whose band directors were *not* trumpet players. In fact, Johnson often said that when he started teaching at the University of Northern Iowa his trombone students initially improved more than the trumpet players. This was because he did not get as involved in equipment and the "deadly trap of over-teaching." It is more effective to teach fundamental ideas than "trumpet jock stuff." Concentrate on relaxed breathing, sound, and shaping the phrase, and work on these things constantly.

Emory Remington couldn't play after World War II but instead sang in all of his trombone lessons. Get the sound of singing in your head. Flood your mind with the music, with the sound that you want. When you let go, you're singing through the horn. Similarly, when someone asked Arnold Jacobs what he talked about when teaching a young student with no real problems, Jacobs responded, "Don't talk about anything. Play!"

As performers, it is best to use the simple, creative approach. Good ideas are the stimulus for the good sounds you want to produce. You can't consciously control the muscles to the fine degree needed for musical performance. The subconscious mind is better at control, and more capable of subtlety and nuance. Concentrating on the desired musical result will guide the specific physical adjustments needed.

The analytical approach is also valid, and, as a teacher, you have to do some of both. You have to know what a student is capable of sounding like and what changes are necessary. You should talk to the student in terms of ideas that will conjure up the best responses. If a student is very tight in the throat, don't call his attention to it: "Put your hand here, can you feel how tight that is?" Instead, direct his concentration to the sound. Shake his shoulders for relaxation in a holistic, rather than isolated, way.

If the student misses a high C a few times, don't mention it. Focusing on a problem exacerbates it, which limits and narrows the response. Tell him that what is really important is the vibrato; nine times out of ten, the C will be there. Give your students something positive to do.

Instead of dealing with a problem head-on, it is best to work with solutions. Learning to play an instrument is not a process of eliminating the bad, but of doing a few things better and better.

Basic Concepts: Sound

The most important musical skill to develop is listening, and its chief manifestation is the idea of how you wish to sound. It is impossible to perform a skill unless one has a very clear image of it. Sound is an aural image. A concept is something conceived mentally, something you create. You can play with consistency only what you hear clearly in your mind. The single biggest indicator of how well you are going to play is how clearly you have formulated your ideas.

Johnson encouraged students to think of sound as all the details that could be heard in a musical performance. Hear your desired sound, first in terms of pitch, then articulation, volume, timbre, taper, vibrato, on so on. It is the aural concept that directs your physical efforts in playing.

Speech and music performance are closely related. Your language and accent match what you have heard. A child in Britain will sound very different than one in Texas, although they are both speaking the same language. When learning to speak, you assemble sounds in patterns that fit the environment. No knowledge of the physiological or neurological processes involved is necessary. To use this approach in teaching, take in the sound, then practice reproducing it. This alters most brass teaching. Start with the desired sound rather than, "Do this." The student must have a focus—the product. If we taught people to speak the way we teach everything else, we'd have a silent society.

Apply the ideas behind language acquisition to your teaching. We will sound like those players to whom we listen the most. Part of the reason that little Johnnie sounds pinched and nasal is because the only players he has heard are the kids sitting beside him, who also play that way. The teacher should expose students to the "language"—the characteristic sound of the instrument and good musical performances.

Suzuki students learn to play before learning to read music, and their listening skills are often better than those of some college students. The sound is the music; the notation is not the music. Just as we are fluent in our native language before learning to read, we should be guided by the sound we want when playing. The notation is just a reminder, and at best a blueprint, of the sound (in all of its elements) that we want to express.

Practice thinking musical sounds in as much detail as possible. Correct pitch and rhythm are only the starting place. Develop the skill of inner hearing so that the sound is always in mind. Don't segment your thinking; you're an entire, whole entity. Labeling things or trying to tell each part of your body what to do breaks down the functioning of the entity. Thinking instead of the sound operates the whole system, so guide the playing by sound rather than by feel. Don't create an awareness of physical feeling when you play. Feeling is subjective and can be misleading, so it's not a good way to judge performance. Thinking of the sound you want will call up whatever you need that day.

At times, the instrument can be a distraction. Introduce simple physical habits away from the horn. For example, breathing can be taught by using the syllables "oh" and "toh." This approach triggers the correct responses until they become conditioned and dependable. Also work on correcting mistakes away from the instrument. Having students sing a troublesome passage can pinpoint misconceptions of pitch and rhythm, or it can reveal the extent to which the student is (or is not) audiating details such as dynamics, vibrato, intensity, and other aspects of the desired sound.

Question: What do you do with a student who won't sing? When you know you're doing the right thing, keep at it; be courageous and persistent.

Singing can be very awkward and embarrassing for some students, and they want to avoid this at all costs. Students can also be very single-minded, to the point that nothing can get in the way of what they want. This is when empathy from the teacher is important. Mouthpiece buzzing can be an acceptable substitute for singing.

When studying in Chicago, Johnson was told that many of the fine players who had performed with the Chicago Symphony could be divided into two groups: those who could call up new concepts like putting another record on a turntable, and those who had to go home and practice. As players, we need to be able to hear what we want to change and do it, without having to adjust all the dials.

Playing requires reproducing the sound in your mind first. You are dealing with two instruments, the one in your head and the one in your hand. The one in your head determines what comes out of the one in your hand. Ideally, virtually all of what you think is sound. Be a musician who plays the trumpet.

Basic Concepts: Listening

After explaining the efficacy of the natural process of learning though imitation, as well as the importance of hearing and recalling all aspects of the desired sound, Keith Johnson always emphasized the critical importance of listening. He believed that this crucial aspect of music study is much too important to be left to chance and should be guided by the teacher, encouraging all to teach listening as an improvable skill.

Johnson's views are described in detail in the appended article, "Teaching the Art of Listening," published in the *ITG Journal* of October, 1981. Some of the important points are as follows:

- All other skills depend on the ability to listen well.
- Ear training is the most important part of your musical training; it guides everything you play. Solfege is best. Ideally, students should have a sight-singing and ear training lab that requires singing an hour a day throughout their school years.
- The purpose of our work is to create better musicians and better listeners, no matter what class we teach.

Teaching a student to listen can be compared to teaching a child how to talk. The student should hear the desired sound clearly before trying to reproduce it. Repeat it for him as often as necessary in an environment of patience and encouragement. The atmosphere in which an idea is presented is often as crucial as the value of the idea itself. If presented in a hostile or confusing way, the effectiveness of the idea is negated.

In learning to play (or speak), there will be a lengthy "sorting out" period. Things won't work perfectly the first time, but keep repeating for the student. He must gain the ability to hear an idea clearly in his mind before playing it. The sound itself contains all the information the brain requires to reproduce it. Hearing it enough times will guide the student to reproduce it correctly.

Question: How do you get a student to listen more? Play for them—not every etude, but set an example in the warm-up. Let them hear good playing and get that desired sound in their head. People can figure out technique, but they have to hear sound. The best way to teach vibrato and different styles of articulation, again, is to let them hear good examples. Expose them to good sounds. Do all that you can—play a reasonable amount in lessons. Johnson didn't play in unison with students but rather demonstrated passages from material they were studying. Playing duets with students is also highly recommended.

Encourage your students to listen to recordings and live performances. The more experiences you expose them to, the more likely it is that one of them might prove to be the key. Johnson was seventeen before he heard a live orchestra, but he always remembered the first orchestral recordings he listened to: *Till Eulenspiegel*, Tchaikovsky's *Piano Concerto No. 1*, and Rachmaninoff's *Piano Concerto No. 2*. The orchestral performance and recordings made him want to be a musician: "There's something out there that I want to get to."

Work as much as possible on sight singing and melodic dictation to be a better brass player. Sing in your students' lessons; this will help you, too. It's never too early to teach listening. Start with matching pitches on the mouthpiece. Do some ear training during the first five minutes of each lesson. It is a skill that has to be practiced in order to improve. It takes time to develop, and it may develop very slowly, but don't give up. Emphasize listening and singing in every lesson.

Sing the first note of an excerpt before playing it. You don't aim at a target blindfolded. Also sing entire phrases. Practice the skill of inner hearing by audiating your ideal performance of a passage, not only in terms of pitch, but all other aspects of sound. It is the sound that directs your physical efforts, and the more detail you can hear in your mind, the more consistently you will perform.

As another example, listening and singing can guide improved playing in the upper register. Brass players often think of range in terms of up and down; we associate higher notes with a feeling of reaching up. Instead, think horizontally. Listen to how you sing an ascending interval or phrase—there isn't that much physical change in the mouth, jaw, or tongue. Playing the passage again immediately after singing it often results in less physical effort and greater ease of playing.

You can learn much about articulation and expression by listening to singers. Be smart enough to understand that there is a transfer. For instance, the more shades of articulation or types of vibrato you notice, the more colors you will have on the palette for your own playing. Listen more to performers outside of your own area. Listen to the King's Singers. Compare Boston's string section to Chicago's. Also expand—don't cut back—on brass music. Listen to the best, because it helps you in whatever you play. Through listening, learn to know where the composer's heart and mind are, and this too will guide your performance.

Basic Concepts: Breathing

While listening is the most important of all *musical* skills, the most important *physical* skill for wind players is breathing—the use of the air. We spend 80–90 percent of our time attempting to improve this. Many difficulties in range, embouchure, flexibility, intonation, and endurance, are caused by improper use of the air.

For most playing problems, start by looking for ways to improve the air. Don't get sidetracked by "exotica" (as Johnson liked to say), but concentrate on good listening and breathing. If the breath is full and free-flowing, everything else functions better: "We are magicians; we turn air into sound." For string players, the key is the bow arm, not the left hand. For brass players, our air is the bow. Think in terms of motion—air in motion, always moving, either in or out. Static air is bad air.

In each phrase, we must also deal effectively with a continuously changing relationship between air flow, the amount of air moved through the instrument, and air pressure, or compression, with more effort required to expel air after the player has used approximately half of the available air. This issue further varies by instrument. For example, tuba and flute have maximum air flow rates with low compression. On the opposite extreme is piccolo trumpet, for which the air flow is greatly reduced and the compression is much increased.

The problem with playing in the high register of many instruments is that the air flow can shut down as pressure is increased.

Although knowledge of the physical process of respiration is not necessary for fine performance, teachers of wind instruments can benefit from an understanding of the fundamentals of pulmonary function. In a broad sense, two groups of muscles are involved in breathing: those used for inhalation, and those used for exhalation. A muscle has only one positive function—contraction. It works in only one direction. To return (relax), the opposite muscle has to contract. However, the diaphragm is an exception. It is a musculo-fibrous membrane and has no opposite. The diaphragm has to do only with inhalation, almost nothing to do with exhalation. To "blow from the diaphragm" is not possible; its function is to allow air to be drawn into the lungs.

Some players are taught to blow with isometric tension—the so-called hard belly school of brass playing. However, the effort of unnecessary muscular contraction actually reduces the motion and fullness of the air stream. The isometric tension makes it feel as if you are working harder, but the result is less air. Try this with a breathing bag or respirometer and see what added tension does to the amount of air you can move. Johnson felt that Kleinhammer's description of respiration for brass players is quite good.[71]

The left lung has two lobes, the right lung, three. Over this is the sternum, attached to the ribs. The floating ribs (the two lowest, attached only to the spine and not to the sternum) come around from the back. The intercostal muscles cover most of this area from front to back and help inhalation by raising and expanding the chest. Directly under this area is the diaphragm.

In respiration, the fifth cranial nerve sends signals to the diaphragm that cause it to contract downward. The lungs are drawn down, increasing their capacity and lowering the air pressure. Thus, breathing is based on the principle of equalization of air pressure. In other words, air fills the lungs until the pressure is equalized. To quote Aristotle, "Nature abhors a vacuum."

A natural elastic recoil occurs when you inhale. After a full breath, a large proportion of the ensuing exhalation is due to this recoil, also known as the stretch reflex of the lungs. This elasticity allows the player to move a good deal of air without much extra effort.

Vital capacity is the amount of air you can exhale, measured by spirometer. Women usually have 2.5–4.0 liters; men, up to 6 liters. Residual volume refers to the amount of air always left in the lungs; you can't completely empty them.

With respect to vital capacity, you can't change what is inherently there (just as you cannot change your height). You can develop what you have, and you may be underusing what you have already. As you get older, your lungs lose a little elasticity.

The tidal volume, which is the first one-half to one liter of air, comes out quickly and efficiently. After this, you get into the expiratory reserve volume, which takes more effort to move. Although you can never expel *all* the air in your lungs, as you approach the last of the air you *can* move, it takes more work to propel the air and maintain a consistent volume.

Good Respiratory Practices

When we play, it is common to start with "frog to tip" breathing for the first phrase, but throughout the piece we often gradually decrease the amount of air we take per breath, using just the middle of our "bow." Breathing efficiency doesn't automatically remain high; either you continuously work on it and improve, or you get complacent.

The best way to teach good breathing is to use the sounds "Oh" or "Ah." Making the proper sound ensures all the right physical responses, and it is easy to use and to remember. As with other skills, teach breathing with broad, general concepts and focus on the product: the sound of a good breath. This approach gets better results than giving physical instructions about what to do with the diaphragm and chest muscles. We play best when we think creatively, not analytically.

Have your students aim the air at something external, rather than just at the lips. Blow a piece of paper at arm's length, at a curtain, or at a match. For higher notes blow faster, not harder. Encourage them to think of higher notes as further away, like a ladder lying on the floor. Don't allow students to hold air with the glottis before releasing. Tell students that the air does a U-turn, going in and out without a pause.

Johnson avoided using the terms "breath support" or "breath control" in his teaching. Support holds something in place, and it implies a stationary position. Telling a student to support or control the air stream usually results in abdominal stiffness. The connotations are ultimately harmful. There will be some positive muscular effort for a "high x," but don't let students add tension in anticipation. Teachers get better results and state things more accurately when they talk about blowing and air in motion.

To approximate the feel of playing the higher instruments, try closing holes while blowing through a spirometer. For piccolo trumpet, learn to keep the flow going without unnecessary tension. You must maintain air flow even with enormous compression. Sometimes an intelligent student who lacks the ability to sustain high compression will make a good low brass player.

Improving Breathing

Good posture is very basic to wind instrument playing but is often overlooked. Arnold Jacobs told Johnson, "There's nothing wrong with your breathing. Don't be lazy, sit up straight and take a good breath!" End of discussion. Correct posture is usually taught in early lessons and is often taken for granted afterward. Students need to be reminded to sit tall by reaching up with the crown of the head. Think of length and relaxation. There should be a gentle curve in the lower back.

To help establish good breathing habits, use a breathing tube. The three-quarter-inch size is suggested, because it is the size of a person's trachea. When using larger-diameter tubes, the jaw will close up in the back, and using a smaller tube can be too restricted. Just put it in your mouth, and you will see that you can't take a bad breath.

The breath should be smooth and without friction, but not totally silent. Six good breaths every day will improve your breathing and stabilize it at a higher level. With a student or with yourself, you must be very conscious of the use of the air; check it periodically. Don't neglect to work on breathing, but actively seek to improve it as long as you play.

It is also helpful to ask students to imagine taking a bite of very hot food. This "pizza breath" moves as much air as possible across your tongue. This lowers the tongue and brings the air in with less tension.

The more air you take in, the more efficiently it comes out. Use a toothpaste tube to illustrate: if you want exactly one inch of toothpaste, it comes quite easily out of a full tube. A nearly empty, squeezed tube will require much more effort to get the same amount of toothpaste out.

Students sometimes take in a large amount of air, but don't expel it all. This leads to excessive tension and after a few such breaths, they have to exhale before taking in air for the next phrase. Encourage such students to "waste the air; try to run out." The goal is maximum flow rate for increased efficiency and better tone production.

When students have played too much the day before and complain of being stiff, spend several minutes working with a spirometer. This more vigorous use of the air will make a surprising difference in the response of the lips when they start to play. This reminds players that air fuels the playing process, regardless of how their lips feel that day.

For soft playing, simply blow less vigorously. Don't lock or clamp down on the air column. A soft dynamic is not a negative dynamic. Think of riding a bicycle: you can pedal slower or faster, but both are a positive action. Likewise, you don't "put brakes" on the air in order to play softly. Blow freely in a positive way at the appropriate volume.

Additional Concepts

Articulation: Fundamentals

Articulation for brass players occupies the same role as diction for singers. Brass articulation can be divided into two categories. The consonant "T" is used for harder sounds, and "D" for softer sounds. Other possibilities are "L" and "N." These categories overlap, and each contains an enormous variety of strength, character, and sound. When changing from normal articulation to a more legato or staccato style, alter your concept, just as you would in pronouncing a word with a different emphasis. Put differently, don't concern yourself with the physical changes; instead, think of the sound you want.

The ways in which you can articulate are as infinitely varied as in speech. For example, the articulation can be thought of as the equivalent of the consonants in lyrics. Think in terms of subtleties and shading. The mind and body are so subtle in control, expression, and creativity that you can do almost anything you can conceive. There are many aspects to this, which can be very frustrating because the possibilities are endless, but it stays exciting and challenging because there is always more to do. The primary activity you must engage in is *listening*.

To understand the possibilities of your playing, listen far beyond the confines of your instrument. Listen to Dietrich Fischer-Dieskau and other fine singers for their diction. While the text provides instruction for singers, as brass players we must choose articulations based on what we infer from our sense of the character of the piece. Our articulation is a form of inflection; it gives clarity and character to the musical message or meaning. This is a far cry from "tonguing."

Most of the time, poor articulation is caused by poor air, which is to say that, in actuality, tonguing problems are rare. Air is the root cause; tonguing is the symptom. The tongue simply goes up and down. The stroke can vary in strength and rapidity.

Again, work on problems away from the instrument. Take a deep breath and make sure the air is flowing. Play long tones and make sure the sound is good, big, and full. Say or sing the sound you want, with a very long and sustained sound (though not necessarily legato). Next, blow the air pattern on the hand and then play it on the mouthpiece. Last, go back to the instrument, focusing on that sound and emphasizing air flow. If something isn't working, it is probably because of excess tension. Improving on this requires time: let the student work out of that tension.

For any skill, learn to determine how long you need to work on something with a student to be effective. With a young student, for example, it defeats the purpose if you go past his attention span. Give him some mental "fresh air." Focus on tonguing for a few minutes, then go on to something else. Later, you can return to the idea for a few more minutes.

Some teachers designate an exact point in the mouth for the tongue to strike. However, since facial structure is unique, Johnson felt it was foolish to prescribe the same point of contact for every player. As a starting point, the tip of the tongue hits near the spot where the top teeth and gum connect, but this is a general guideline, not a rule.

If there is inadequate air, tension sets in. Muscles respond in sympathetic reaction. Tension is systemic and usually starts in the respiratory system. When the tongue is relaxed, it can operate with incredible speed and finesse. If there is a lack of air, the tongue tries to compensate by urging the air out from the back of the throat. This makes the throat tight and puts the tongue too far back.

See the Arban book: the syllable "tu" in French is pronounced more toward the front of the mouth.[72] It requires more finesse and dexterity. The American "too" or "tah" may put the tongue a little too far back or too low to produce the best sound.

There is a shifting balance in the relationship between the strength of the air and the strength of the articulation. The fullness of the air doesn't change. Always use as much as possible for the dynamic and pitch required. It is the strength of the articulation that changes. For legato, the tongue stroke is light; for marcato, a stronger and more vigorous articulation. Never lighten up on the air; alter the strength of the articulation. Soft playing is almost a pure breath attack. The air is responsible for starting the sound, the tongue for its definition.

Rapid passages are often printed with dots, especially in French music. Consider staccato to mean well-marked rather than spaced. Ghitalla taught: "The faster you go, the more legato you have to play regardless of the indication." Play the notes very fully. Use the strongest articulation you can while still keeping up. Try this in Rimsky-Korsakov's *Scheherazade* and similar literature. The legato stroke is shorter and, with the "du" syllable, the tongue is lower and doesn't have to move as far.

When playing something with lots of tonguing, be certain that the emphasis is on sound, flow, and line. If a student plays a phrase that sounds choppy, have him practice it slurred. Then blow the same passage, adding a light articulation while keeping a focus on continuous air flow. Don't "try to tongue"; instead, blow the air very freely, and just let the tongue touch it. Tell your students that "the air blows the tongue out of the way." Aim for the best sound. As in other physical skills, get the student to think in terms of the sound he wants in his articulation. This guides all that you do.

Articulation: Initial Attacks

Problems with initial attacks are a common malady of insecure players. Hesitating before an attack builds up pressure and can trigger the Valsalva maneuver. Cultivate and practice the following: all attacks are essentially breath attacks, and it is the breath rather than the tongue that makes the lips vibrate. Think of the breath as making a U-turn rather than conforming to an "in-wait-out" pattern.

If problems occur, practice lots of pure breath attacks. We should teach ourselves to depend on the breath to make the lips vibrate, and then add whatever articulation is called for. In most situations, our articulation should emphasize the vowel rather than the consonant. Sometimes illustrating this by contrasting "t**OH**" with "**T**oh" will help clarify it for a student. In a sense, all attacks are breath attacks, with some articulated and some not. The key is a good, unfettered breath. Hesitating introduces tension, which lasts throughout the phrase.

As brass players, most of our missed notes are on the high side. Initial attacks are a part of our work on accuracy, which depends on good listening and good tone production. Look for basic solutions; when we miss on the high side, it's usually tense production and poor hearing at fault.

Symphony players sit a long time and have to come in cold. You must be able to hear the first note of a passage. Try to hear it as literally as possible; flood your mind with the sound, as if you're listening to a recording. This helps develop a strong sense of relative pitch.

Teaching students to "breathe, set, play" starts bad habits. Don't attempt to consciously set for a note, because the time it takes is really very small. Instead, tell students to "blow the air out before you stop taking it in." There should be no hesitation, like kicking a football. Edmund Cord of Indiana University recommends that you breathe in on the same pitch you will play. Also, practice breathing in the same style in which you will play, as a violinist does on the upstroke of a bow.

Take two breaths before playing. The first one "clears out the cobwebs" and lets all the tension go. The second breath turns air into sound. Breathe vigorously; this gives more motion and volume to the air and is more relaxing. Tell students to blow faster, not harder.

Articulation: Multiple Tonguing

Double- and triple-tonguing are used when you can't single-tongue fast enough. The single tongue is the model, goal, or standard—make the substitute sound like the original. Get the "tu" sounding as good as possible using the four steps of sing, blow, buzz, and play. Keep the air nice and long. Use the same four steps for the "ku" syllable. Play slowly, with a healthy volume and long notes.

When teaching, work on this over a period of time. Spend five or ten minutes on it at a time, and come back to it once or twice during the lesson. Emphasize listening; the player should focus on how he sounds overall: air, sound, line, relaxation, listening.

When double- or triple-tonguing, people often play too fast, which just masks problems. Slow it down to hear what you are really doing. Make sure the attacks are clean and the notes long. Speeding it up is the easiest part. Use the same four steps: pronounce it, blow, buzz, and play. You may have to spend a great deal of time on each, over several lessons. If any step doesn't sound right, go back to the previous level.

It will be necessary to remind students to keep embouchure firm. The corners will tend to get loose when concentrating on multiple articulations. Think forward, especially for the "ku" syllable. Avoid having an interruption, as in "tu ku/ tu ku," where the sound stops between each note or pair of notes. Also, take care that triplets don't become three sixteenths. Make sure the first note is long enough.

Johnson recommended practicing the alternate syllable in all positions, so it is as flexible and natural as the "tu." However, he personally did not use displaced double-tongue pattern for triplets, as in: TKT KTK. Although this is logical, he considered it extremely awkward. See page 75 in *The Art of Trumpet Playing* for practice patterns.[73] Do each one slowly and carefully before the next. Also, play Mussorgsky's "Great Gate of Kiev" with "ku" attacks for practice. Anything less than a clean attack always sounds like an outlier.

Articulation: Staccato

In many trumpet method books, staccato is taught quite early. This can lead to very poor habits of articulation. Instead, as Johnson recommends in *The Art of Trumpet Playing*, teach them to play good sounds and phrases before working on staccato. Students should be able to play a succession of quarter notes with a good attack and no space in between notes first. Demonstrate this by passing your hand in front of the air column while blowing a long tone. This is how young students should approach tonguing: blow a long tone and add the articulation. Playing with space between the notes is very sophisticated, too much so for beginners.

Avoid teaching staccato articulation to younger players for at least two years. It is far better to teach them to blow long notes with good releases; don't attempt staccato until this is established. Also, for younger students, "playing shorter" often intuitively means stopping the note with the tongue or glottis, so they must work to develop tapered releases. A vivid image that works with some students is comparing releases to the shape of bullets instead of shotgun shells. Drawing these shapes and demonstrating the tapered bullet release and the abrupt shotgun shell stop works better than long explanations.

Start by working on tapered releases with a series of dotted half notes. Keep the emphasis on tone quality while working for a musical, floating release. Gradually speed the process up, but go back to a slower tempo if the release is not done well.

For more advanced students, demonstrate phrases with different strengths of articulations. Cichowicz often played connected notes with a very heavy articulation, which he called "the impression of staccato." In very rapid passages, there isn't time for actual separation between the notes.

Most students come to school with better technical than musical skills. There is a severe underemphasis on playing musically, while mechanics are overemphasized. Get the student listening and thinking musically. Teach them that what they want to create should determine what they do. Muscular and neurological abilities may often have been misdirected, but the body is still capable of what you're trying to accomplish. Directing one's efforts toward a musical goal often yields immediate and dramatic improvements in technical ability as well.

Flautist Marcel Moyse used to say, "There are no technical problems, only phrasing problems." If you understand the tone quality, sound, shape, and articulation of the phrase, then you can play it. Start with a sense of the whole. Begin teaching musicianship from the first lesson by working on line, phrase, and flow rather than on stopping notes.

Braces

Johnson taught many young students in Iowa and came to two general conclusions: first, braces are a problem, and second, they are often more of a problem when removed.

Trumpet players with braces are encouraged to try covering them with rubber, paper, wax, or the various commercial products available. However, it is likely that nothing will prove entirely satisfactory. Ideally, let the student take some significant time off, although this is not always practical. When playing with braces, the student may need to slightly adjust the position of the mouthpiece or try a larger one. There is no good answer.

Be supportive and encouraging. Don't pressure the student, but reason with him. It's not the end of the world to play second or third part. You should have a sympathetic and compassionate manner to help them get through it.

When braces come off, they can become an even greater problem because the rules change all over again. Work together with the student, parents, and orthodontist. Try to time the removal for the beginning of a hiatus, like winter or summer break. Don't touch the horn for at least a week, or longer if possible. Get rid of all the old physical feelings. In effect, the student is starting all over, so make sure that it is done correctly. This is better than returning to practice the next day, when there may still be sensitivity or pain.

Johnson recommended having the student start practicing again on a daily basis, for a few minutes a day for a week, then twice a day for two or three weeks. Start by working on breathing exercises. Next, form an embouchure and play long tones on the mouthpiece. Work for a full, rich sound. Expand the range until the student is going up and down by a third. By the end of the week, they can start playing very simple tunes.

Start all over again on Monday of the second week by returning to breathing, single pitches, and easy songs on the mouthpiece. Then add very simple material on the horn, such as exercises by Getchell and Cichowicz. By then, the students are usually on the right track. Keep the reins on, and check every step to spot problems. Don't pound a wrong approach until it feels right. Johnson's article in the *Getzen Gazette* explores this topic in greater detail.[74]

Embouchure

The "embouchure" refers to the lips and facial muscles that are used in the playing of a wind instrument. The function of the embouchure is to focus the sound and determine the color. The air is actually more important than the embouchure because it is the air that makes the lips vibrate, and the size of the air column passing through the lips determines the size of the sound. Johnson often said that, in all his years of teaching, he had seen only about a dozen real embouchure problems. What he meant is that most conditions are not problems with the lips but symptoms of the real problem: air. The embouchure is primarily an instrument of response; it needs to be positioned well, and then the air makes it work.

Embouchure is important, but the more you talk about it, the more likely the student will become concerned with it. So, keep things in perspective. Decide strategically how to get what you want from the student.

The embouchure should be resilient, flexible, and strong. It needs to be in a state of relaxed firmness. It should be firm enough to focus the pitch, but not so rigid that it won't move. Remind students that forming an embouchure is like having a live bird in the hand: the grip should be firm enough to hold it, but not so rigid as to hurt it.

To form an embouchure, say "tu" and push gently on the corners with the thumb and index finger. Close the lips by humming, then *blow* the embouchure open. Don't set it open; the lips should be touching, but not stiff. Both lips should vibrate. The top lip is the primary source of vibration, and the bottom lip vibrates sympathetically. Initially, you should center the mouthpiece, but allow for individual variation over time. Trumpet mouthpieces are often a little below center, while other brass instruments use more upper lip.

The teeth should be reasonably aligned. Try to get the student's jaw position in or near this position, but if it doesn't respond readily, don't force it. Haynie felt it was very important to get the teeth aligned, while

Johnson concentrated more on warm sound and flowing breath. However, saying "oh" brings the jaw forward, so the two approaches converge in a similar result.

When working on embouchure, remember that good breathing is absolutely the first priority. Start beginners on the mouthpiece for a couple of weeks if possible. Also, insist that beginners start on cornet. Don't let them pull the horn in and down. This pushes the lower lip over the teeth and shuts off the vibration. Show students the "brass player's face": corners firm, making a V or U down to chin. Put index finger over lips down to chin to remind them. Work on the direction of the airstream. Blow on the hand. Have the student think about where you want to aim the air, rather than what's happening physically (such as moving the jaw forward).

Some students of Johnson, Cichowicz, and Jacobs tend to play in a manner that is a little too flabby overall. This may be due to all the talk about relaxation. To avoid this problem, keep the embouchure firm all the way to the bottom of the register. If firm and focused, all you have to do is open and close the aperture. Again, the primary purpose of the embouchure is to focus the sound. Imagine the aperture as a hole blown open like the lens of a camera. You want to change the size of the opening, but not its shape or character.

Achieving the right amount of tension in the brass player's face can be guided by listening. If the low register is billowy and uncontrolled and tonguing is difficult, or if when going from low to high it sounds pinched, squeezed, and sharp, then the embouchure is too relaxed. Some players add tension in the throat to focus the sound, which can result in glottal noises. This also can open the aperture too much, causing the sound to be diffused, fuzzy, and airy.

Test yourself: start with a middle C, and get the best, fullest, most focused sound that you can. Play down the scale, keeping the same sound that you started with, and then play Clarke Study No. 5. Also, get set to play high C, drop the jaw a little, and then play low G. The resulting pitches should be firm, focused, and responsive. It's the same embouchure; the difference is the aperture and air, not in the amount of firmness.

The best lesson on embouchure is to look at the pictures in Farkas' *The Art of Brass Playing*.[75] All the embouchures shown have a good, muscular setting and are strong and flexible, but each is unique. As teachers and as players, we should operate on principles, not rules. Your goal is to get the best sound as easily as possible.

Flexibility

In trumpet playing, flexibility is the ability to move around the instrument freely, quickly, and smoothly. The main ingredient is a freely blown sound. Motion to the breath is needed so you can move up, down, and around. The air, embouchure, tongue, and fingers must be well coordinated. Flexibility implies the quality of fluidity: moving gracefully and elegantly. Style should be emphasized; the speed can be no faster than the style allows.

To slur on valved brass instruments is to move from one note to another with absolute connection of sound. There should be no break or separation. To eliminate unwanted intermediate notes when slurring a large interval, ask students to play a glissando or smear on the mouthpiece and "make it real messy." When we play the same slurred interval on the instrument, we just speed up the smear until the extra notes are no longer heard. Put the emphasis on the connection. Have the student concentrate on keeping the air going, even if there are extraneous notes in the early stages of practicing slurs. This is a good start and is better than stopping the air to avoid the other notes. Teach your students to think of a fluid slur, rather than notches or stairsteps for the best connections. Even in the most rapid slur, think melodically.

Philip Farkas would record a clean slur on a reel-to-reel tape recorder and play it back at half speed to allow people to hear the glissando and the desirable effect accomplished by how the air is moving with no breaks. The best way to practice slurring is on the mouthpiece. The Crisafulli interview in *The Instrumentalist* also contains good information on the use of the mouthpiece for improving slurs.[76]

One of the greatest maladies in brass playing is using the throat and tongue to control the air flow. This results in glottal sounds and notched notes. Don't try to use syllables such as tah-too-tee for the different registers; motor skills cannot be controlled that way. The vowel sound should always remain the same: "oh." The tongue arch does change slightly, but using different syllables can change the shape of the embouchure. Guide yourself by the desired sound and keep it consistent. You do normally want the sound a little brighter as you go higher, but overuse of syllables takes a naturally occurring phenomenon to a ridiculous extreme, as in the pivot system.

Have young students work on lip slurs a great deal. Demonstrate by playing a siren on the mouthpiece. Start with a fifth, and play a big smear in slow motion. Look at Pat Harbison's *Technical Studies for the Modern Trumpet*, which is based on Clarke Studies and other methods, and you will see that it doesn't overemphasize syllable changes.[77]

For flexibility, think in terms of air flow. For higher notes, blow faster and farther away. For lower notes, the air slows down. The tongue floats inside the mouth and the aperture changes, but these adjustments are subconscious. Problems occur when the throat is restricted, because then, when the aperture is too open, you get a blatting sound—what Johnson jokingly referred to as the "Frick and Frack brothers."

Think of trills as rapid slurs. Each note should be clear. Be sure that the embouchure is firm enough for the upper note. When playing whole- or half-step trills with valves, form your embouchure for the upper note and let the valves do the work for the lower note. For lip trills, start by playing very clearly and slowly, and think melodically. Problems begin when you start too fast, and then you get impurities. The pitches close in, with the low note sharp and the high one flat.

In performing rapid slurs, think melodically and nontechnically. Good musicianship always results in better technique than thinking mechanically and trying to calculate physical functions. Actually, we get the most efficient mechanical operation when we're producing the most musical sound.

Intonation

For good intonation, three things are critical: a well-developed sense of listening, good tone production, and rhythmic stability. When listening to yourself, the objective is to "get out in front" and hear yourself, not worrying about pitch to the point where you're afraid to play. Stopping the wheel on a tuning machine and playing in tune have little to do with each other. Be relaxed and critically objective while listening to yourself. You should give constant attention to pitch, but not let it spill over into tense production. In this sense, a tuner can do more damage than good. Get students to listen to themselves without being afraid. You can't play in tune without both good listening and good tone production.

Play simple duets with your students; look for melodic pieces with lots of fifths and octaves. These perfect intervals will produce a resultant tone when played in tune. Guide the students to listen for this. Deliberately teach students the difference between good and bad pitch: play a fifth with the student, bringing your note in and out of tune, and tell them which is preferable. Work on pitch in a nonthreatening way.

When tuning to a piano, play your note first. Get a big, full sound and hold it until you have it in your ear. Visualize your pitch on a line. When the piano plays the tuning note, your eye will jump up if the piano's pitch is sharp and move downward if the pitch is flat. So many times, we listen to the piano first and lip up or down to match it. Instead, when tuning, we need to adjust the length of the tuning slide for any discrepancy in pitch. Consider a player who listens to the piano pitch first and lips up to match his tuning note to the piano. He will have to play the entire piece with this extra effort, and endurance is greatly decreased. When in doubt, put the slide where it belongs and make sure that you are playing easily and with good tone production.

This good production is a another aspect of playing with good intonation. Once students have been taught how to take a good breath and play freely and in a relaxed manner, after a few months you can also start working on matching pitches. If you have an older student who is playing with unnecessary tension, it's best to work on improving production first, because this tightness prevents the natural resonance that is the starting point for the best pitch. Good tone production and good intonation go hand in hand.

Sometimes it is necessary for a director to make adjustments from the podium, but ideally we should take a longer view and work on fixing the player. Work on consistency and learn to play your best seven days a week. Herseth had good and bad days, but on a bad day he was still better than anyone else.

Rhythmic stability is also an important factor for intonation. Uncertainty hurts tone production. In this regard, using a metronome can solve both pitch and rhythmic problems as Johnson often related in reference to an experience he had in a quintet rehearsal. A passage in a Holborne piece presented many difficulties for the group, and one member suggested trying it with a metronome, saying 'at least the rhythms will line up.' They found that the intonation also improved markedly when they played with the metronome. If you know when to play, you will be able to coordinate your physical responses.

Much of what you teach can be dealt with while instructing two students at a time, as long as they have no problems. Play duets and emphasize having fun. Your students (and you) should practice for enjoyment, not out of a sense of duty. Your students should want to practice, and peer pressure is often greater incentive than playing for the teacher. For this reason, more often than not, where there is one good player, there are two. This is also one of the advantages of going to a big trumpet school. The element of competition can be a great motivating factor.

When teaching, go long on enthusiasm, energy, and spontaneity. Don't talk about intonation too much and too soon. Just plant a seed and let it grow. Use a holistic approach; you want the player to improve as a package. Talk about a nice, warm sound: "waste the air."

Later, using a B.E.R.P. (buzz extension resistance piece) will take care of the center and focus of the pitch as well as reduce extra tension in the mouth and throat. Use the tuner and tape recorder as starting points to create self-awareness. You learn to play in tune by listening.

Some equipment is better in tune than other choices. Johnson at first chose based on the sound, but later considered intonation to be the first criteria for picking instruments and mouthpieces. In his opinion, on C trumpets, a 25H leadpipe has a good sound but horrendous intonation. Once a choice is made, stop worrying about it and get busy practicing with it.

Motivation

Why do you play? Why do you practice three to four hours a day? What motivates you? Students can be motivated by example and encouragement. As a teacher, you teach by what you are, more than by what you say. Therefore, you shouldn't plan to practice less later on in your career. Rather, continue working to reach your own level of excellence. Maintenance is not enough; improvement must be ongoing in order to continue over a thirty-five-year career.

What you are teaches the most. To serve as a motivator, you must be motivated yourself, and the music itself is the best source of motivation. Listen to really good recordings after students' lessons, if needed, to regain your aesthetic excitement. Remind yourself why you are going to practice. Like a stonemason building a cathedral, you may need to step back occasionally to get a better perspective. Together, the individually chiseled stones take on more meaning. The small individual part is not as critical as how it fits, and the whole is lessened when your part is missing.

During the course of a career, little things can tug away at you—imagine Gulliver among the Lilliputians. When the system grinds you down, go back to the music, the source of your inspiration. If you end up going through the motions—not practicing much and just playing in lessons—your students will pick up on this. Listen to the Chicago Symphony, get better sounds in your head, and raise your level. Remember that what is in your head determines what comes out of the instrument. Don't forget the music!

Playing isn't enough; only listening gives a sense of the whole. Turn on the radio while you're driving. Make music listening part of your life. Ask other people who they listen to (Herseth listened to Swedish tenor Jussi Björling). In the orchestra, you may be playing a dog trumpet part, but you should still listen to the piano concerto being performed; you've got the best seat in the house.

While the music itself is the strongest motivator, as teachers and as players we need to seek and provide many types of motivation. Sources of motivation can also include encouragement, colleagues, and successful experiences.

With respect to encouragement, the best way to teach is to find out where the student is and build from there. Don't tear down or pick apart the student or his playing. As Crisafulli said: never discourage a student. Cichowicz liked to say that every student has a measure that he can play as well as André. It is the teacher's job to find that measure and build from there.

Don't tell students what they're doing is wrong, because that will not help them to get better and improve their confidence. Instead, give them very concrete things to do, and they'll remember what you want. This, rather than thinking of all the things they did wrong, gives them more confidence for when they perform. Be encouraging and start with what they *can* do.

Colleagues are another source of motivation. Associate with people who are musically alive. One of the advantages of top schools is being around a number of determined students. In a small school, that kind of dedication is rare. When teaching at such schools, you have to create that interest and light fires under people, and this takes an enormous amount of energy. Usually, however, where there is one good player, there will be more. The students can motivate each other and get people excited about playing.

Successful experiences also inspire people. The first performance has to be a positive one. If a student folds, it can scar him for a long time. Don't put a student onstage until he's ready. As confidence develops, the student should play for an audience as frequently as possible until being onstage feels normal. Have your students play for each other in masterclasses and public performances. Also encourage them to think of their lesson as a public performance.

The key to confident performing may be playing early enough, before a student becomes judgmental about his own playing. If a student is already anxious, don't put him onstage if he doesn't have a chance of doing well. It is better to play a simple piece very well than a challenging piece unsuccessfully.

Think through your views and adapt to each student. Get to know each student personally and establish a relationship. A few people play better in public, so give them something a little harder. Most students, however, should be given an opportunity to experience success with an easier piece before going on to harder literature. Exploit their strengths first; later, assign pieces that build weak areas.

For graduate students and others who are auditioning, when a job is on the line, pretty good is not good enough. It is better to play something less difficult than to fail nobly.

Mouthpiece Placement

There are three physical facets of brass playing: the breath, the articulation, and the embouchure. The embouchure is the most difficult to guide musically. A change in the embouchure (including the placement of the mouthpiece on the lips) doesn't show up with the same immediacy as a change in the air. The embouchure requires coordination and muscular development. Changes for the better don't always sound that way.

Johnson recommended a generic approach to mouthpiece placement. For trumpet or cornet, start with the mouthpiece ap proximately centered, both horizontally and vertically. Allow for individual adjustments. The best way to tell if it's correct is by how it's working. It is a nebulous gray area, so establish guidelines and listen to the sound.

Real embouchure changes, in which the mouthpiece is repositioned, are rarely necessary. The teacher should consider two questions: How old is the student, and what are their future plans? Estimate how far the student could develop, with and without the change. Gauge the frustration level relative to how long the change will take and what will be lost. In most cases, a fifteen- or sixteen-year-old who is not going to play beyond high school shouldn't be changed. It takes away the pleasure of playing.

Changes in mouthpiece placement should never be made for the reason that "it doesn't look right." Instead, listen and judge the student's progress on that basis. If things are improving at a normal rate, don't interfere with it, because students play the way they do for a reason.

However, often the student will progress to a certain point and stay there. When there is poor flexibility, focus, range, or development, a change may be necessary.

Telling a student to change his embouchure can be like saying "cancer." Most changes can be made without mentioning the word. Saying that "you can't do anything until …" is nonsense. If a student does need a change of mouthpiece position, introduce it in a nonthreatening way. Demonstrate for them by playing a tune on the mouthpiece, moving it to a different setting for each phrase. Then set your mouthpiece where it normally goes and say, "It sounds best here, because this is where I've practiced it." Tell the student (and the director), "We're working on it and I'm giving you exercises that will help. We're going to work on breathing, good sound, and other things that will make the embouchure work."

Be tactful and persistent. To change a situation, you have to get inside. The best subversive is the one in the three-piece suit. Win the confidence of the director, student, and parent. Establish yourself as a person of knowledge and character. If they don't have confidence in you, it doesn't matter how much you know.

Mouthpiece Playing

Playing the mouthpiece is a singularly important technique—in this, Keith Johnson declared himself to be a disciple of Arnold Jacobs. You get the best benefit when the mouthpiece is played in the most musical way possible. Everything you do, from the first breath to the concerto, should be musical.

Buzz the music and play freely, even if you miss a note. Don't make it cautious, studied, or tight. Start with the trumpet solo in Stravinsky's *Petrushka* or another well-known passage. Don't play as if it's a true/false test; just take a big breath and go. Use this time to set up the approach you're going to use for the rest of the day.

Most players use the mouthpiece early in the day but understand that the warm-up is neither separate from nor different than playing; they meld together. There should be no dichotomy between the way we warm up and the way we play.

Mouthpiece playing indicates how well the body and mind are working; it maximizes efficiency and directs the responsibility where it belongs—to the player. It makes you aware of any lack of full, rich air flow, because it is easier to recognize on the mouthpiece than on the instrument. Playing the mouthpiece also improves listening; it clears up inaccurate or out-of-tune passages amazingly well. Valves only get you in the vicinity, while the pitch is really made by the player. In the long term, mouthpiece practice helps to develop the ear. It also helps develop a sense of line and phrasing. Start with simple tunes and easy material where you sound the best.

Using a B.E.R.P. can make a dramatic difference when the focus isn't good; it gets you to listen and move the air. Johnson recommended using the mouthpiece for extended excerpts, songs, or systematic studies such as Stamp's *Warm-Ups and Studies*.[78] Use the B.E.R.P. for isolated passages as well; it focuses attention on moving the air and hearing the pitch.

Buzzing the mouthpiece also increases endurance. Take a few good breaths and play aggressively. Buzz Stamp exercises up to C and D "faithfully but not carefully." Regular practice is necessary for any real improvement, but play or buzz freely rather than trying to avoid mistakes.

Also buzz melodies, excerpts, and familiar melodies on the mouthpiece. Playing the mouthpiece has a very stabilizing influence. Many young professionals have a high level of artistry but a low level of consistency. When you buzz, do it well, not mindlessly, like mumbling a rosary. Playing the mouthpiece raises your minimum level.

When using the mouthpiece, give yourself the freedom to miss notes. Show off, "think Hollywood," and play exuberantly. It doesn't matter *what* you buzz and practice, but *how*. Play enthusiastically with a big sound. Practice playing expressively. Practice telling a story.

When traveling, play the mouthpiece for ten minutes at a time, two or three times a day. This will keep you in good enough shape to easily get back into regular shape in two days instead of several. Buzzing smooths the transition back to playing. Chicago Symphony brass players would take their mouthpieces with them on week-long fishing trips.

Mouthpiece Pressure

Mouthpiece pressure is essential in playing a brass instrument. Excessive pressure is not a problem—rather, it is a symptom of a problem. You should have just enough pressure to seal off the embouchure, because you need to have contact to channel the air. The problem is usually lack of firmness in the corners or not blowing enough air across the embouchure. Again, go to the source. Teach the student how to take a good breath and how to buzz the mouthpiece with a firm embouchure.

For piccolo trumpet, the mouthpiece pressure needs to increase along with the air pressure and the air speed, because this helps support the smaller aperture. The question of what amount of mouthpiece pressure is excessive is subjective, but buzzing on a visualizer can force you to form a correct embouchure.

Pedal Tones

Pedal tones can have a therapeutic, relaxing effect when played while focusing the embouchure and blowing aggressively. Don't worry about the sound or musicality. Use lots of air, play rather loudly, and stay relaxed. There should be no tension in the shoulders or in the air stream. The muscles have to be in a state of relaxation to receive enough blood and oxygen to recover and strengthen. Thus, pedal tones speed up the process of relaxation. Another benefit of practicing pedal tones is learning to use large volumes of air, thus improving the motion and flow.

Performing as a Career

As professional performers, brass players must have a confident, positive attitude. When onstage, think about the music, not yourself. Always think musically and don't get sidetracked with technical or mechanical problems. Concentrate on how the piece sounds—that is, how you want it to sound. Don't worry about mistakes, past or future.

Your preparation must be long-range and cover all situations. Your warm-up and daily practice routine should be comprehensive and rigorous enough for mastery of the material and to build up endurance. Always have the music prepared ahead of time; never sight- read in a rehearsal.

Practice concentration above all else. As Johnson liked to say: "Practice as if you were performing; perform as if you are practicing." Proper practice will build confidence, consistency, and musicianship as well as technique. So, spend a good deal of your practice time on material you can already play well.

For solo preparation, start well in advance. Look over the piano part and make sure the accompanist can handle it—if not, change either the piece or the player!

For ensemble performances, study the whole piece with score and recordings to know how your part fits into the whole. Notice style and tempo variations, as these are not always indicated on the part. Work out difficult sections slowly and carefully until they seem easy. Make sure the transposition is completely worked out and that you can be rhythmically confident.

Do not be intimidated by a conductor or other players (they may be as nervous as you). Enjoy performing. Treat playing your instrument as a hobby you love, not as a life-or-death matter. Do not allow doubts to creep into your thinking. Play aggressively, with no concern for mistakes. If you make an error, forget it! Later, work it out in practice.

If things aren't going well in your practice, don't panic. Back off from the problem, if possible, and rest. Look for simple solutions, such as tension or lack of air flow, rather than complex, exotic problems. Remember, everyone makes errors. The biggest offense is not a technical error but a dull, lifeless, inhibited performance.

Trust your body. Don't let yourself get tense and substitute isometric tension for positive air flow. We sometimes sabotage ourselves with unnecessary extra effort. Allow mistakes to happen without being overly concerned or overreacting.

Both physical and mental changes must occur if progress and improvement are to take place. When insecurity (mental anxiety) leads to physical tension (rigidity), the desired change is inhibited. Fear stifles thinking, concentration, and constructive thought. Physical tension inhibits the subtle adjustments necessary for different ranges and tone qualities.

The "natural" player thinks in terms of concepts rather than how to play, while the "mechanical" player is concerned with function. For example, we don't think of "how to" play loud; we simply play loud! Think of the musical sounds you want rather than giving yourself verbal instructions. You can imagine that it is someone else playing and trust your body. Self-confidence comes with an understanding of the total process of playing and by trusting your body to perform a few basic skills, which have in large part been learned away from the instrument.

Pivot System

The pivot, in which the head or jaw goes in the direction of the pitch, is a natural occurrence for most players. It keeps the air going straight into the horn and takes the pressure off the upper lip when going higher. There is also a reverse pivot, found in those with an occluded jaw.

A little pivot is normal and desirable. Tell the student, "as you go lower, drop the jaw," but don't push it. Attempting to consciously control the pivot can result in excessive movement and create problems. If the student is a good player making normal progress, leave it alone.

Practicing

Put yourself in the proper frame of mind. Be quiet for an entire minute and think of what you want to accomplish. Have definite goals; seek results rather than just putting in the time. Think in terms of principles; listen for the sound instead of "learning the notes." Take something and change it in a substantive way. Do it better (not higher, faster, or louder). Each day in your mind, define what constitutes "better": sitting taller, breathing deeper, playing more musically, etc. Practice to improve the fundamental things. Johnson once spent an entire hour with Jacobs on one line in the Arban book, working on sound, intonation, and breathing.

Good playing consists of doing the basic things better and better for as long as you play. Don't get bored and let peripherals replace song and wind; this is more important than everything else put together. Take a deep breath and sing through the horn. This is simple, but not simplistic.

Your practice must be *comprehensive*. Cover the fundamentals: sound, line, range, articulation, transposition, etc. Students should practice at least three hours a day, but it varies individually and according to one's playing schedule. Ideally, practice time should be broken up into short sections. Cover all technical aspects as time allows. Do not allow yourself to become frustrated. Know when to rest and when to stop.

Your practice should be *intensive*. Concentrate on really changing something. Don't go on until it is noticeably better.

Practice *regularly*—as Johnson liked to say, "only on the days that you eat."

Start with your warm-up routine. Get the fundamentals working as well as possible. Have definite objectives and put your music in order. Jacobs said one- to two-thirds of your practicing should be on music that you already know. This way, you are improving your musicianship, because you can listen more carefully to how you really sound.

Melodic playing is essential to developing good listening and good air flow—two of the "big ones." Play easy, lyrical material without the music. Think of difficult passages as being melodic. Think of *all* passages as melodic. Melodic practice takes your mind off yourself and focuses it on the music. This can be very useful for working out problems. Playing "tunes" one has known and played for years is *very therapeutic*.

Work on a good cross section of material. Don't get muscle-bound in a single area. To work on a certain technique, zero in on it and then give it a rest. The learning process continues in the mind. Later, come back to it. Practice things more often, for a shorter amount of time. Don't try to learn something in two days. You can damage your playing by over-practicing due to fear and urgency. Also, study the music without your horn. Practice efficiently in short periods: sing, and solfege it, to get the music in your head. You have to "own' the music.

Problem-Solving

You are your own most important teacher—you teach yourself how to learn. Try to teach yourself with the same disinterested, objective involvement and concern that you would use with a student. Stop, put the horn down, and think of what you would say to someone else. Think of specific ways to make a passage better, instead of just trying it again. Back away from it from time to time. Think in terms of "what I have accomplished this semester," in the same way that you would view your students' progress.

When teaching yourself, be objective! Listen to how you sound. Don't judge by how a performance feels, because feeling is highly subjective and misleading. Set definite goals, such as a larger breath or a smoother intake or exhalation. Spend plenty of time on simple materials, working on fundamentals.

When problems develop, look for simple, basic solutions. Air flow is the most common failing because it is affected by such factors as apprehension, fatigue, or insecurity. Be careful to distinguish between serious problems, minor annoyances, and minor annoyances that you *think* are serious problems. Avoid exotic answers, for they are rarely ever correct.

If problems persist, stay calm. Stop—think about what you are doing. What would you tell a student in such circumstances? Consider what you have been practicing. Step away from practicing for a time (and the more severe the problem, the longer you should rest). Try to work out the difficulties using simple material you know very well.

The most common minor problems include inconsistency, lack of endurance, and poor coordination. These are most often caused by physical or mental fatigue. Realize that, while the physical requirements of trumpet playing are usually exaggerated, mental concentration is far more likely to be the problem.

The best way to work out problems is to go back to basics and play simple material. Sometimes, problems are brought about by practicing too much advanced material without enough emphasis on basic, simple skills.

If serious problems persist, get to the best teacher you know as soon as possible. Trying to solve major difficulties that develop in your playing is not unlike an ill person trying to cure himself—very foolish.

Range and Endurance

Almost all students mention range and endurance as areas of concern. To develop these aspects of playing, the player must start where he is now. First explore the range in which you can play very well, then gradually extend. The high range is no different than the other registers; you use the same principles of full breath and good sound, just blowing faster. Be skeptical about shortcuts, whether physical or mechanical. Johnson recommended that his students read *Mind, Muscle, and Music.*[79]

We often tend to think, talk, and worry about range without practicing it. As the embouchure develops, students should work on the higher register, even if the initial sound is not the best. Not even middle G sounded good when we started. Play up there until it improves. Go after the right kinds of things, seeking to achieve the best sound before going even higher. The more musical you make it, the easier it will be physically. Above all, seek to play musically.

Johnson's method book for range development uses beautiful and melodic material to take the player into the upper range.[80] Clarke studies are also very good. Don't try to *hit* high notes; rather, strive to play beautifully in the upper register. With young players, let extended range evolve naturally and intelligently; don't label it or set limits. Develop the whole package.

Most of the trouble with playing up there is mental. When a student has trouble, have him buzz without knowing where he is. Tell your students, "I don't work on the high register, I work on trumpet playing." There is often much more good sound inside us than we let out.

As a player, recast negative thinking about high range or anything else. Raise your level of concentration, but not your level of tension. Auralize Herseth playing it beautifully, then try to play what you hear. An idea is only as effective as the way it is presented, so express what you are saying as clearly as possible and in a positive way. Deal with solutions: "here is how to do it," rather than "avoid this." Crisafulli never said anything negative. At the same time, you have to be rigorous and can't ignore problems. Get the student's mind focused on doing something in a free and positive way. Instead of saying, "This is really hard; work on this passage," say, "Let me show you how to make this easier."

The teacher's job is to start where the student is and build from there. Don't let him leave with things taken apart—put them back together. Show him what is needed and how to work on it. A player who is afraid to make mistakes will never reach his full potential.

Endurance, or how long you can play, is really a by-product of good practice habits. If you practice well for regular and extensive periods, endurance increases. Better breath, sound, and focus to the embouchure will help you to play longer, so practice to truly improve these things. Don't just extend your practice time; learn to play *better* for longer periods of time.

There are both mental and physical aspects to endurance. Why can we play a piece in practice but not in performance? Anxiety and tension are often the culprits. Mental tension leads to physical tension. Sometimes, however, physical tension exists independently, especially in young players. Muscles react sympathetically. Being tense in one area can lead to overall tension, resulting in a lack of air flow and a tight embouchure.

No substitute exists for thorough and correct practice. To strengthen musculature, practice must be interspersed with periods of rest. Enthusiastic students sometimes over-practice to the point of sounding worse or even bruising the lip tissue. Many fine brass teachers recommend resting as much as you play during a practice session. You should finish each session stronger than you began.

The more you think about endurance, the less you will have. Don't baby yourself in an effort to get through a piece or a concert; do what you're used to doing. Keep your mind on the music. There is a difference between playing intelligently and holding back. View your practice and performance as a job: this is your routine, not something that interrupts your routine.

Stage Fright

Much of stage fright is misplaced ego. It says that we are thinking about ourselves and what the audience thinks. To the degree that we get our minds on the music and off of ourselves, the problem of nerves is lessened. The edge from adrenaline ought to be there, but it should work for you, not against you. It should pump you up and help you to play with more energy.

Mistakes are a part of the learning process. Instead of discouraging them in a young player, accept them. If the object is to avoid mistakes, then the product becomes sterile. Your music should tell a story; you're an actor with an instrument. Don't build a fear of mistakes. When Herseth missed a note, it was a bloody mess. Trying to avoid cracked notes is no way to get anywhere. Play to make music!

In many lectures and lessons, Johnson advised students: "Be well prepared, and know that you are. Then get onstage as much as possible. Practice concentrating on the music in less stressful situations. Concentration for a comfortable performance is a skill that can be improved by practice."

He also emphasized the importance of visual and aural imagery: "Picture yourself on stage. See yourself the way you would like to look while performing. Try to hear yourself giving the best possible performance: hear what it sounds like in detail."

Finally, he advised arriving early for performances and warming up on stage. Check out the lights and the acoustics and, in general, get accustomed to the situation. As much as possible, rehearse where you're going to perform. Acclimate to the environment. After you've done all your preparation, your mindset can be: "just play it one more time."

At the beginning, there is nothing commonplace about a performance situation, so it is normal to be nervous. You will grow more confident with exposure to the situation. Robert Elworthy, former horn professor at Indiana University, has put it simply: "It helps to be prepared." Crisafulli was once asked a long question about how he would get himself focused, knowing he was about to go out onstage and play a major work with one of the greatest brass sections in the world ... and he replied, "Sometimes, I eat an apple." So, in your preparation and performances, be serious—but not obsessed. Johnson advised musicians to put all their performances on the same level; all are equally important, and the music deserves our best.

For teachers, having a student start over at every mistake can be very damaging. You can get the same effect by turning on the tape recorder without losing musicianship. We should also bear in mind that we can be falsely conditioned by commercial recordings. They are highly edited, and the elements of excitement, energy, and humanity can be lost. Tell your students: "I don't want you to play perfectly; play musically," or "make it exciting." We're looking for art, not perfection.

Beta blockers are a crutch for performers struggling with stage fright. Some people may need them, but teachers shouldn't make recommendations, only a physician should. Prescription medicines should not be tried until all other techniques have been used.

Stress

Conscientious people are sometimes their own worst enemies. When we allow ourselves to become tired, this can lead to stress. It can affect all performers, but type A personalities seem especially likely to experience stress. It can take as long to correct the situation as it took to build it up in the first place.

Burnout is easy to see in others, but harder to recognize in ourselves. Be aware of the signs: insecurity, lack of motivation, and bad attitude. If you begin to experience stress, back off. Adjust your schedule to stay fresh. Professional brass players aren't always able to practice three hours a day while performing, and advanced students and young professionals should plan accordingly. Ideally, we should balance our performing, practicing, and relaxation.

Some musicians take a day off every week, but Johnson didn't recommend this for brass players. Brass playing is more demanding, in terms of muscle tone and stamina, than piano or string instruments. Although the fingers don't forget their technique, the embouchure can decline in only a few days.

Learn to get more done in less time. Plan your practice in such a way that you are fully prepared well before the first rehearsal so that you can be physically fresh for the performance. Excessive last-minute practice can beat up your face until you lose sensitivity and response. Mentally, allow yourself to be calm and objective. Don't be so concerned with what you do that you don't do it well. Balance is important.

Studio Teaching

There is a place for hard work and putting yourself on the line, but the ability to step back and view your work in perspective is also important. In Johnson's first lesson at the University of Illinois, Haskell Sexton took him out for a beer.

Start the lesson in a low-key manner and put the student at ease. Take a few minutes for conversation unrelated to the trumpet. Remember that you're not teaching the trumpet—you're teaching the student. If the teacher is abrupt and businesslike from the outset, it can negatively affect the student's playing. Throughout the lesson, remember to present your points in the most positive way possible. The atmosphere in the lesson or conversation is just as important as the value of the ideas expressed. Trumpet playing should be enjoyed, so talk about how much fun it is.

Next, start with a few basic things: breathing, mouthpiece playing, flow studies, Stamp warm-ups and so forth. This gives both you and the student a sense of how the system is functioning. If something is not working well, it is easier to fix at this stage. Cichowicz said that trumpet playing involves taking a deep breath and singing through the horn. Jacobs coined the phrase "song and wind" to describe the same idea: the body will consistently produce sounds that are clearly heard in the mind, and the air fuels the playing process.

Guide the student to his best level of playing on these few basic things before progressing to more difficult music. In the long term, this approach will teach him how to get the best responses from himself. Johnson constantly reminded his students, "You are your own most important teacher." Hard music is simply fundamentals put together in quick order. Initially, a difficult passage can seem like a video game, where many bullets or enemies are flying toward you all at once. Teach students to look at one measure and break it down into simple parts. Encourage them to approach it in a calm, thoughtful manner.

Remember that students are often nervous in lessons, especially at first. Part of your job is to put the student at ease. In the early stages, it is useful to observe the student's anxious reaction to public performance. Slow things down and help him learn how to deal with his nervousness. The teacher has a decided influence on the situation. Your manner can leave a student tied up in knots or help increase his confidence.

After a negative experience, try to guide the student to a change of attitude. Get him to the point where he looks forward to lessons and practicing again. Sometimes, it can take up to two or three years of "unteaching." Keep trying to change this for the better.

Have unlimited patience as long as the student is working. Some very serious and committed students simply progress more slowly than others.

Creativity and imagination are very important, but many students tend to be quite literal. Guide them to think in abstract terms: tone color, shades of articulation, types of vibrato, and so forth. Help students to develop their imagination. Ask them to think about things, such as: "How can you make it more exciting?" Or, ask them to play the same phrase twice: make it sound like a march the first time and a lullaby the second time.

When mistakes occur, rather than telling them they're "wrong," find ways to redirect their efforts. For example: "I liked the energy; let's see if you can get a better attack there, too." Don't cause students to withdraw. Your purpose is to refine their creativity, not stifle it. Allow students to experiment and to develop a real sense of style.

Work to develop players who are well-schooled but still distinctive. They should play with a full sound, a singing line, good intonation, and rhythmic stability. They should also have transposition skills and the ability to recognize and play in different styles.

In many teaching situations, it is often assumed that a phrase is correct if it gets the right response. It is better to make sure that the information is also correct, rather than passing along old wives' tales. We tend to trust what we read, as well as teachers we admire, especially if they are fine players. However, certain brass anthologies and method books contain a large portion of material that is worthless or harmful. Be iconoclastic: question ideas and think them through.

Teachers must be very careful with what they say, especially to good players. We want to get the truth across and have them understand things correctly without interfering with what they are doing. Reorient the student slowly.

There are two good tests for any recommendation:

- Is it good information? In other words, is it reasonable and based on the best research? If not, be skeptical. It is all right to question authority. You needn't reject everything, but don't accept it blindly either. Like playing out of tune, after a while anything can sound okay.

- Do you find the idea usable? It should be expressed in such a way that you can incorporate it into your playing. It must be reducible to a core—not simplistic, but simple. The best ideas are musical, simple, and effective. This is the connection between the beginner and the advanced or professional player. The more advanced one becomes, the more simple the approach. You can make anything complex, but that doesn't meet the purpose. For more on this subject, see the article "Basic Skills for Young Trumpet Players."[81]

Teaching young kids is much the same as teaching doctoral students or professional players. Although they don't use the same music, there is no *essential* difference. You may use longer words, or discuss ideas in greater depth, but you are working with the same concepts. The difference in the players is not in exotica, but in how well they do the basics.

Good playing is not a matter of learning complex ideas and details but of learning to use a few concepts and skills to an ever- higher degree: listening, breathing, embouchure formation, and articulation. Professionals work on fundamentals throughout their careers, applying them to increasingly demanding situations. Learn to look at difficult music in terms of basics: take a deep breath and sing through the line. Break it down into simple elements.

Always play music, not exercises. In this regard, there can be an undesirable dichotomy in our approach. Sometimes we *practice* scales and long tones, and then we *play* music. Johnson's dog would lie quietly at his feet while he was warming up but would start howling at the opening of Mahler's *Fifth Symphony*. This made him realize that he was not approaching all material in the same way. We never "play scales" in a symphony or a concerto; therefore, we should *always* think of and play a musical line. So, don't just practice scales; play them as musical lines and require a beautiful sound from yourself. Treat the Cichowicz flow studies as musical lines too. The idea is the same whether you're playing "Long, Long Ago" or the Haydn *Concerto*.

Learning about physiology is fine, but not in the lesson. In the studio, you should focus on how you sound rather than on intercostal muscles or the embouchure. As a teacher, you look, listen, and observe, and then you find things to say that will change the response. As a performer, you'd be dead in the water doing this. You must think differently when onstage, because your task is to tell a story. Jacobs would say, "Take off your teacher's hat and put on the performer's hat. Those are two different jobs."

Ear training is vital. Young players often have had no training, and college students don't always connect the sight-singing and dictation skills in theory classes to their work on the instrument. Because you can only play what you can hear, ear training must be taught, practiced, and developed. Don't neglect this. Take some time in lessons for ear training, and remember that it must be related to the student's performance.

In addition to pitch and rhythm, players should be able to hear orchestration, balance, color, subtlety of attacks and releases, vibrato, phrasing, and intonation, in solo as well as ensemble playing. Have students listen to fine players, and guide their listening as their skills develop. This takes much time and work.

Transposition

Transposition is a purely intellectual skill, not a musical problem. It gives you mental flexibility and improved ability to concentrate. Transposing by clef is more efficient, but for trumpet and horn transposing by interval is probably more common. Start with very simple melodic material that the student already knows, so that he will recognize any errors. Use easy etudes, popular tunes, and melodic studies. Rather than tackling many transpositions at once, focus on one transposition, such as trumpet in C, until the student is very comfortable with it, and then go to another common transposition. Low brass players must learn to read clefs fluently. Again, start with one at a time.

Always work out the part ahead of time; never sight read in an orchestra rehearsal. Also, don't write out your transposed parts—learn them by memory! Conductors should never know that you are transposing, because that is your responsibility. Treat the rehearsal as a performance; practice is what you do at home. A professional orchestra does six or seven performances a week—the last four are *public* performances.

University Positions

A terminal degree is usually required for a tenure-track college teaching position. Although there are exceptions to this, they are increasingly rare. Larger schools and prestigious conservatories are more concerned with the playing ability and experience of prospective studio teachers than with their degrees, and many of the best-known brass pedagogues do not hold doctorates. First jobs for young people today, however, are rarely at top-tier institutions, and in today's market, it is wise to complete a doctorate if a college position is your goal. Working with talented and motivated students is an attractive feature of university teaching. Colleagues are also a source of artistic and scholarly stimulation and can be one of the most enjoy able aspects of the job. Work to build good relationships as diligently as you work to build your program.

Entry-level jobs often require a variety of activities such as studio teaching, directing ensembles, coaching chamber music, and teaching brass methods or other courses. As a new instructor, you should be prepared to teach in related areas. Peruse the vacancy lists to see which combinations are commonly advertised, and stay awake in your music history classes!

When applying for a job, follow instructions to the letter. Include whatever materials are requested, but nothing more. Particularly, do not send recordings until requested. Have a high-quality recording ready to go, and be sure that your letter of application, curriculum vitae, and any other documents requested are well written and without errors. Ask two or three people to proofread your documents for you.

In order to sustain a long career, it is most important to stay connected to the music. Studio teachers should put performing first. You have to be very diligent to practice, perform, and listen throughout the course of your career. You will have many other duties and expectations in a university position, but don't let anything else crowd out the music-making. By reading, continuing your own studies, and attending conferences and workshops, you can keep the spark alive. Plan to practice and improve for as long as you play and let the music itself motivate you.

Vibrato

The basis of a good sound is a beautiful straight tone. Vibrato is a musical ornament, an embellishment or enhancement, giving a certain characteristic to the sound. Vibrato is an oscillation of the sound, but the core or center is consistent. Good vibrato fits the style and does not call attention to itself. It adds a finish to the sound, like a final coat of varnish. Vibrato is not the substance of the sound.

Practice without vibrato often. Make the straight tone all it can be, and only then add vibrato. Don't try to use it to project the sound or to mask bad pitch. The sound has to be blown out freely. Develop the sound, and give the students good examples of vibrato as a basis upon which to form their own concepts. Listen to Helmut Wobisch playing Haydn with virtually no vibrato. Practicing this way is useful because it shows you what you're *not* doing with the sound and the phrase. Practice a few times without vibrato, and then allow it to work its way back in. Vibrato should be an integral part of the sound, meaning that you shouldn't notice it. Too little is better than too much, so be conservative.

Vibrato can reveal a player's national background. For example, Guy Touvron has a vibrato similar to André's, due to a common experience of listening and music-making. Vibrato, tone quality, and articulation can help you identify national trends:

- German: least vibrato
- French: narrow and fast
- Russian: wide and fast, even for horns (listen to Leningrad)
- British: more sedate, not as much vibrato

American vibrato has slowed down since Herseth. Roger Voisin and Armando Ghitalla had a faster vibrato. The tendency among American orchestral players to play in a less soloistic manner has become very influential. Many consider the Chicago Symphony brass section to be one of the finest in the world.

There are several categories of vibrato. Section vibrato should be just enough to warm up the sound, a little added intensity. This is not heard as vibrato, but rather as just a tad more live than a straight tone. Sometimes a bit more can be used in the top voices. Soloistic playing uses a greater variety of vibrato.

Vibrato can be produced in different ways: externally with the hand (or trombone slide) or by means of the so-called diaphragmatic vibrato, in which the air stream is altered. Sometimes, the latter is done by the throat. Vibrato can also be produced in the oral cavity with lip, jaw, or tongue movement.

Johnson preferred hand vibrato on trumpet, but most people use a combination. Teach hand vibrato first because it doesn't interfere with, or regulate, the air column. It is easy to see, control, and stop. Do whatever works to get appropriate speed and width. The fluctuation should be both above and below the center of the pitch. Do not allow students to substitute vibrato for good production and good intonation.

Work with the player on moving lots of air; talk about wind in motion. Problems with vibrato are usually due to tight air flow. You may have to teach this step-by-step to a younger player. Play for them and give them listening recommendations to help them develop an idea of good vibrato. Be able to produce the sound you want, with the control you want. Like an accent in speech, it comes from inside.

Keith Johnson's most memorable lesson on vibrato was when John Haynie told him, "You've got the worst vibrato I've ever heard. I've told you everything I know, and it hasn't helped. Go fix it!"

Warming Up

The value of a warm-up is great in both the physical and psychological aspects of brass playing. It improves our confidence and stability and raises the amount of oxygen through the increased blood flow. The lips are the area we focus on, and they are second only to the brain in the amount of blood supplied. There is actually not much warming up to do for the lips; a Bronx cheer will do it. As far as the lips feeling good, this is mostly a matter of air supply.

The warm-up is not as physical as we think, but it is still very important. It is the time in which we set musical goals and connect the mind to the tissue.

The level to which we do this when we begin to play will determine how well we play that day.

A warm-up is individual, so adapt it to your own needs. It may take from three to thirty minutes. Johnson felt that spending forty-five minutes to an hour on the warm-up is excessive because that's a big chunk of your playing time. Be as musical as possible. Blur the line between the warm-up and "real playing." Apply the same standards of sound and production to the warm-up. Play vigorously and freely—it's not a true/false test.

Missing your warm-up is not a physiological problem. Although a good a warm-up develops confidence and dependability, you should be able to live without it. If you must, you can walk out onstage, pick up your horn cold, and play. Jacobs sometimes had advanced students start their lesson by playing excerpts and solos with no warm-up to show them that this is possible.

The most important time in your warm-up is the first moment or two. Be still and quiet for one minute to stop and think about what you want to accomplish. Keep in mind the big breath and the sound that you desire. Play comfortably but also fully and freely. A suggested routine may include the following:

- Breathing exercises: these are so important that, without them, the other things don't matter. Stimulate quantity and freeness: air in motion.
- Mouthpiece playing: make it musical. Play Cichowicz, Schlossberg, zippy little tunes, Clarke and Arban solos, and other literature. Play exuberantly, show off, and don't be afraid of hurting your lips.
- Long tones: Move around, don't take a note and hold it, because music exists in phrases. Get to the point where you don't need the music, so that you can listen to yourself play. Use Cichowicz, Stamp, and similar music that contains "moving long tones."
- Technical studies: Clarke, etc. Treat these as flow studies. Cover the whole book twice a week. Play warmly and musically, and turn each scale into a piece of music. Move around on the horn. Belfrage studies are also good, and you should play one or two a day.
- Melodic playing: Use Rochut, Concone, Bordogni, Getchell, Kopprasch, and Balasanian. Play with a singing sound and learn to listen to yourself. Do some of this kind of playing every day.

- Pedal tones: perhaps right after mouthpiece practice. These are good, but not indispensable.

These are very broad categories. As needed, you can omit, modify, or add techniques such as articulation. The routine should vary a little, so that you don't become mentally numb. Find several books and studies in each category to accomplish the same purpose without it getting stale.

Don't neglect the upper register. Work on it early in the playing day when fresh. Work in short bursts: a few Clarke studies or one line played four or five times. Then rest, and let it grow. The next day, it will be better.

Cultivate mental determination. Control your body with the mind so that you will be less dependent on the physical warm up. Thinking about the desired sound determines how well you play. You can, by exerting the power of mental concentration, control the way you play.

Coda – Music as Metaphor

Johnson's second book, *Brass Performance and Pedagogy*, includes an essay on "Music as Metaphor," in which he describes his evolving realization as a teacher that, although not all of his trumpet students became professional performers, their time together was never wasted.[82] He gradually came to the conclusion that music study and participation was a metaphor for other aspects of life. After the book was published in 2002, Johnson continued to expand on his thoughts about this topic and included additional ideas in his later lectures. The following information is taken from Johnson's handwritten notes and has not been published.

Not all students will pursue performance as a profession, but for all students music can be a metaphor for much deeper values. The habits formed in the study and practice of music become part of one's lifestyle and can be the pattern for gaining other useful skills.

The intrinsic value of the music itself is also of great importance, and all students can develop an appreciation for music and art beyond that which they produce themselves. Creativity and an appreciation of aesthetic values are important to education and for leading a meaningful life.

The influence of art in our society is both provocative and civilizing. Bach, Mozart, Beethoven, and Mahler express the deepest feelings of the human condition. This is not limited to music. Poetry, drama, and dance are also wonderfully expressive. Painting, sculpture, and architecture have left us with many masterpieces to contemplate. Works of literature such as Shakespeare and the King James Bible have greatly influenced our modern world.

Educational studies have shown that strong arts programs have a stimulating and cultivating effect on students. Mental and physical development are enhanced, along with practical skills and desirable characteristics such as poise, decision-making, human interaction, individual responsibility, and commitment to what Johnson described as the common unity.

Trumpet performance is a highly specialized discipline. However, Johnson's seminars covered specific aspects of instrumental music that cross the boundaries between areas of practice (particularly brass, woodwind, and voice, as well as, to a lesser degree, keyboard and strings). That said, what all performers do must be grounded in the full range of human experience. In other words, we tell stories. Think of how you would play or sing "The Star-Spangled Banner," "Amazing Grace," or "Joy to the World." Performing requires the ability to communicate a story and to convey abstract emotions.

We must be advocates for the humanities, which are fundamental to a civilized individual and community. The arts must be a central part in any education because they integrate questions, statements, skills, and productivity. Aesthetic experiences open the door to self-reflection; as Socrates said, "The unexamined life is not worth living." Arts have lasting effects on the individual, the workplace, and the larger society.

Therefore, rather than focusing exclusively on training professional players, teachers should prioritize the following goals:

- Making performance a pleasurable, satisfying experience—neither strictly "a good time" nor drudgery
- Bringing the student to a fuller understanding of the music (style, period, special problems, and historical perspective) as well as a

deeper understanding of the self (whether confident, shy, aggressive, lazy, nervous, subjective, etc.)

- Teaching through a musical approach, whenever possible, rather than a mechanical/technical one
- Freeing the innate musical abilities—of whatever degree—inherent in almost everyone.

Music is basic to life and to a good education. It is not a frill. When teaching music in the public schools, you show your students the benefits and pleasure of music. Draw them to the art of music; it ought to be a part of every person's life. If you expose students to good music, you don't have to tell them how great it is. Just show them the possibilities and the music will sell itself.

Part Three

Reflections

Keith and Cecile Johnson with former students at the International Trumpet Guild Conference in Columbus, Georgia in 2012.
Courtesy of Cecile Johnson.

Encounter

Lines of lives in endless patterns;
Chances gone, opportunity spent in vacuous action.

Surely such chances are not chance,
But encounter always intended.
Some great hand that moves the pawns,
If we but take the move, and act our role.

An *augenblick*, then gone—
What if?
One such precious moment if we
But dare to act,
To be what visions feared.

Restrained by fear,
What glorious moments flee our grasp,
And life if spent while
Still we wait—and ask.

But once or twice in this brief tide,
When courage stiffens and will does act,
The prize of knowing what vectors bring,
Of souls, of spirits, of moments molten
Made to cast;
Is given to us, so swift and fleeting.
And all that is, is memory.

Keith Johnson
25 July 1994

A number of Keith Johnson's colleagues and former students have sent tributes that, together, give us a fuller picture of the man as a dedicated musician and passionate teacher, a gentleman, a scholar, and a delightful human being. Notably, many had vivid recollections of their initial meeting with him—a first lesson, a chat after a clinic, or playing together at a gig—that made a lasting impression. Most of Johnson's associations lasted for decades; his warm friendship extended across time and distance.

He once gestured toward a picture of Vincent Cichowicz in his office and said, "I feel like I owe him residuals." We probably owe Johnson royalties as well as we remember his voice and his warm trumpet sound, center ourselves with a full, relaxed breath, and are inspired by the example he set.

Our encounters with Keith Johnson enriched our lives and will remain treasured memories.

Encomia: Praise from Those Who Knew Keith Johnson

In Fall 2009, my oldest son Cameron was diagnosed with a rare form of leukemia. I ended up spending nine months living in Children's Mercy Hospital here in Kansas City while the doctors and nurses tried, heroically, to save his life. We lost Cam in November of 2010, and I ended up spending three semesters on family medical leave from the UMKC Conservatory, where I've taught since 1989.

Keith was one of the people who taught for me during one of those semesters. To the best of my memory, he was here in Kansas City six to eight times that semester, teaching my full studio of students in packed three-day visits. I found out later that he, quietly, wouldn't accept any payment for his teaching here. I will be forever profoundly moved by that gesture of compassion and kindness, and I think it beautifully sums up his fundamental essence as a person.

Keith Benjamin
University of Missouri-Kansas City Conservatory

My first lesson with Mr. Johnson lasted more than two hours, which I'm sure was due to how much work I needed, but more likely because of

Mr. Johnson's selfless generosity with his time. He continued to commit that kind of care to his students, right up until his last day on the job, and certainly in every interaction I had with him over the course of my three years in his studio.

Mr. Johnson was always a kind, supportive, funny, and uplifting gentleman. Even after his many years as a professional trumpeter and teacher, he had a way of making you feel like you were his most important student. When I called him several years ago to tell him I'd won my current job, he was overjoyed, and it made me feel absolutely wonderful. I still recall that conversation as one of my greatest moments, because I had made Keith Johnson proud of me. I am so humbled to call myself a Keith Johnson student, but I am more proud that I was able to spend time with this man who taught me so much about character and dignity, both as a professional musician and as a human being.

John Cord
Luther College

I met Keith when I was nineteen years old. As a student at North Texas, I was away from my family in Canada and everything I had relied on as a musician. I struggled with my confidence as a young man and as a trumpet player. My anxiety got in the way of the sound I was searching for.

My first impression of Keith was that of a kind and supportive teacher who immediately put me at ease. When I played for him, he noticed the tension that took over my entire body. He put his hand on my shoulder and simply said, "Relax, take a big breath, and play the sound that you hear in your head." The thing is, it was very hard for me to do that. It was only after I had studied with him that I understood what that meant. It was the simplest concept, but it was so easy I couldn't get it.

His words have stayed with me. Decades later, I've finally been able to put his words into practice, not only with my music, but also in other areas of my life. I can face an audience with a work like the Bach Magnificat, and instead of hearing my self-doubts, I can hear the music I want to play in my head. Relaxing gives me the emotional and technical strength I need to bring my interpretation to the most challenging works.

Keith's lessons even found their way into my work as a competitive weight lifter. A relaxed athlete will be able to lift much more weight than one who is rigid and tense.

I'll be forever grateful for his patience, kindness, and support.

Sgt. Jonas Feldman
Canadian Armed Forces

I've been trying to find a suitable anecdote to convey my feelings about Keith Johnson, but there is simply no one story that is colorful enough to describe the essence of my experiences with Keith. However, I can distill my feelings into a set of characterizations about the qualities that leave me a vivid picture of him, what he has meant to me, and what I think he has meant to so many others.

From the first time we met, I discovered Keith to be a gentleman with many other fine qualities. He was highly principled and conscientious, intellectually curious, open-minded. I was always impressed by his ethics and class—fastidious to a fault! Even better words that describe him are integrity and generosity. He always tried to be the best trumpet player, the best teacher and advocate for his students, and always tried to do the right thing every day. He left a legacy for us to emulate.

I am reminded about the late evenings he told me that he had, either to meet students for late-night recital dress rehearsals or the late nights he spent reading doctoral dissertations to make sure his students met their deadline. I am reminded of his generosity in helping international trumpet students and the financial help he sometimes quietly provided. Keith and Cecile showed by their example "how to be," and he left a lasting impression on so many students and colleagues along the way.

Adam Gordon, Senior Lecturer in Trumpet
University of North Texas

While completing my Bachelor of Arts at the University of Chicago, I was both surprised and humbled that Keith recruited me to the graduate program at UNT. Actually, I was quite proud of myself though at the same time I had the distinct feeling that I might have gotten in over my head! Keith met with me after the audition with a Styrofoam cup brimming with black coffee, as was his custom. Somehow, he made me feel not only like was I a fine trumpet player, but that he would absolutely be invested in my future as a musician. When a month or so later Keith called to extend an offer to study with him, the decision was easy.

Over the years, I got a lot of "career stuff" from Keith: a great dissertation topic, an excellent vintage Chicago Monette C trumpet, and a referral to play principal trumpet with the Orquesta Sinaloa de las Artes in Culiacán, Mexico. Most important was his friendship that fueled me with enough confidence to move toward the next level. Keith was there for me through the mundane as well as serious personal crises. The fact I could overcome any of it is a testament to him.

After Keith retired, I brought him to UT-Martin for a recital and to work with my students. His playing was refined and expressive with a beautiful, rich tone – the performance was as strong as I had ever heard him play. He taught with passion and wisdom. And though I'd heard much of it before, the concepts seemed as revelatory as when I first heard them. Perhaps I'd forgotten, or perhaps I didn't get it the first time. My students lit up, and my colleagues who met him were simply enthralled.

Kurt Gorman
University of Tennessee, Martin

It was a great honor to study with Professor Keith Johnson for four years at the University of North Texas, and the time I spent in his studio shaped my life. Those who are familiar with Mr. Johnson's philosophy of trumpet playing know his concept: "Think a beautiful sound, take a full breath, sing through the horn." I am not one of the students who continued with a musical career, but that doesn't diminish what I gained from him. His impact as a teacher goes far deeper and has a much broader reach than just the trumpet world. Not only did he teach me to sing through the horn, he taught me to sing through life. The most important lessons he taught in his studio were about life: grace, being a team player, being adaptable, and always looking for the best in every situation.

A pivotal moment in my life was contracting mono in college and not being able to play the trumpet for six months. I am grateful for the approach Mr. Johnson took with me. He was compassionate and optimistic throughout the entire process. During this time, he taught me the importance of always looking for the good in every situation. As I got closer to graduation, I realized that becoming a professional trumpet player was probably not in my future despite the hard work to regain all I had lost in my playing. Even if I "made it," the very real understanding that a career could be taken away in a flash with an injury or illness led me to explore other opportunities.

I considered changing my focus to elementary music, and Mr. Johnson's wife Cecile graciously welcomed me to observe several of her classes. When I decided not to pursue music education, Mr. Johnson suggested that if I were not playing in an orchestra, I could still work on the operational side of the business. He was instrumental in arranging volunteer opportunities with the Fort Worth Symphony for me so I could get a behind-the-scenes look at managing an orchestra. His foresight to suggest this career option changed my life.

After graduating from UNT, I attended Southern Methodist University and obtained master's degrees in Business Administration and in Arts Administration. I shifted my focus from arts organizations to the larger the nonprofit/philanthropic community. I have been able to help hundreds of nonprofits improve the world around us, something I wouldn't have considered had it not been for Mr. Johnson's vision, compassion, and encouragement.

I say that Mr. Johnson taught me to sing through life because he reinforced the importance of facing obstacles with grace, looking for hidden opportunities, having compassion for others as well as myself, and never giving up. I know my life will be better and more fulfilling by remembering all the life lessons Mr. Johnson taught me.

Allison Davis Hamlett

Class of 2001

I'm grateful for the opportunity to express my appreciation and thanks for my study with Mr. Johnson. I grew up in Waterloo, Iowa, seven miles from UNI. I dreamed of attending school there and was introduced to Mr. Johnson by one of his former students, Denny Vance, with whom I had studied since junior high.

I started my undergraduate degree at seventeen, which I now know is a very immature age. I had heard the jazz bands at UNI and my goal was to play in them. I was not doing well in ear training, and the theory professor pulled me aside one day. I said, "I don't think I really need this." She let me go without saying another word.

In my next lesson Mr. Johnson asked why I was in school. I replied, "I just want to play." He said, "That's great. You should just move to New York or LA, but ..." He then read me the riot act that unless I wanted to do something else in the future, I'd better get going with the theory and ear training. That conversation changed my life. I needed a kick in the pants; he knew that and wasn't afraid to say so.

He graciously allowed me to assist him in the Waterloo/Cedar Falls Symphony, encouraged me to study with Mr. Cichowicz in Chicago, and took me to the brass conference at Roosevelt University where I heard the entire Chicago Symphony brass section and their individual clinics. He encouraged me to compete in the WAMSO competition in Minneapolis where I won third place. I could go on and on. His guidance and encouragement were immeasurable and continue to be so in my career in music. Thanks, Mr. Johnson!

John Harbaugh
Central Washington University

I remember arriving at UNT in Fall 1991 as a doctoral student, a bit scared and overwhelmed. My wife Margaret and our 3 1/2-year-old son Stephen came along for the ride and fully supported my endeavors. It was a challenging two years, but I have nothing but fond memories. Mr. Johnson took me under his wing and treated me with respect. My lessons were absolutely wonderful. He was very patient, encouraging me each time. I always left his lessons uplifted and wanting to practice more – not from fear, but inspiration. His caring and patient approach was just what I needed.

I began going out to lunch with Mr. Johnson and other graduate students. These were wonderful times spent talking about music and life.

The Johnsons invited my family to house-sit for them while they were away in New Hampshire during the summers of 1992 and 1993. For a poor graduate student with a family, this was a delight.

My family also attended the Johnson's church. In May of our second year in Denton, our son Timothy was born. Mr. Johnson had such a profound impact on our lives that I asked him to be Timothy's godfather. Now a young man, Timothy is blessed that Mr. Johnson agreed.

When I encountered challenges at the end of my degree program, Mr. Johnson was there, supporting and lifting me all the way to successfully navigate the degree. He is with me every day in all aspects of life: I could never thank him enough.

Calvin Hofer
Colorado Mesa University

I met Keith on a trumpet course that we gave together in Cornwall, England some 12 years ago. He came to the course with some of his students from the USA and I discovered a teacher who had a very special relationship with these students. There was mutual respect and a modesty on his part that stated to us all that "we are learning to play the trumpet together." A charming gentleman, a fine player and teacher, and with an excellent sense of humour. I am proud to have met you, Keith, and to count you amongst my friends.

Michael Laird
Academy of St. Martin-in-the-Fields

Keith and I had common major influences in our teaching and playing—Arnold Jacobs, Adolph Herseth, and Vincent Cichowicz. We both taught at the University of Northern Iowa and the University of North Texas. We played together in the same faculty chamber music ensembles, professional orchestras, and other musical venues for most of our professional lives.

My son Nathan studied trumpet with Keith during his later years of high school and continued to take lessons from Keith when he returned home after Keith's retirement.

I visited Keith many times after his retirement, and we had wonderful talks about concepts of teaching. He continued to talk in the same thoughtful voice, and in one of our last visits, he said, "Find what works for the student—that is the most important thing." He was the most influential musician with whom I associated during my career as a musician.

Keith Johnson—dear friend, valued colleague, and teacher of my son—you gave us so much.

Donald Little, Regents Professor of Tuba
University of North Texas

My studies with Keith began when I was a senior in high school. He was retired at the time, but he insisted that he was even busier than during his collegiate teaching years!

Studying with Keith was a departure from my previous trumpet lessons. Our focus on more substantive music not only broadened my musicianship, but also helped me focus on playing my best for the music's sake, as opposed to playing my best for competition.

Keith's greatest impact was instilling a relaxed approach to the trumpet. His guidance on breathing, posture, and other physical components were helpful, but he focused on the music above all else. For me, his calm demeanor was more important than what concept he was teaching me. This environment had the most effect on me, and I would often mentally recreate a scene of playing for him in his living room whenever I was working too hard while playing.

At our last lesson, I brought Baylor's ensemble placement audition list so I could get his feedback on the excerpts. One of these was an extended melodic cornet solo from Persichetti's Divertimento for Band. I knew he could help me play it as well as I could.

After the audition, I was shocked to learn I had been assigned principal cornet on the Divertimento. Because I was younger than the other players, I felt out of place at first, but the lesson with Keith laid a foundation that I could fall back on. Performing the solo still made me nervous, but I had played it enough times that tension was no longer part of the picture.

I could focus on making music while singing through the trumpet like Keith encouraged me to do.

Nathan Little, Principal Trumpet
Las Colinas Symphony Orchestra

I came to UNT in Fall 2007 as a doctoral student hoping to become the next great trumpet professor. From the start, Professor Johnson was kind, patient, and wise. He quickly taught me how to be more than a trumpet player and helped make me an educator and musician. Our lessons consisted of pedagogical teaching techniques more than etudes or solos. His knowledge on how to teach was an experience unto itself. Of course, he taught me how to play the trumpet, but what I really learned was the "art of teaching," as he called it.

This is a skill that helped me thrive in several university positions, and which I still use today as a business executive. Even though I left the music profession (for which Professor Johnson would probably applaud), I still draw on the life experiences I had with him. I miss our coffee lessons where we would go to the student union, get coffee and talk about teaching, life, politics, and family. Keith Johnson made the UNT trumpet studio a community that stretches across generations. Thank you, Professor, for guiding us and showing us several paths to walk down. Your lessons will always be a part of my life and I thank you for sharing them with me.

Mark J. Lynn, DMA

One story that stands out the most for me about Keith was discovering he had paid for an entire dental procedure for a student, then finding out it was a French horn player! He had encountered the student during juries and after hearing about the issue offered to pay for the procedure. That was the kind of guy he was. I am certain he did that for many other students, too. I just loved that guy so much. He was always a joy to be around, whether it was at church, or in lessons, or just running into him in the hall. I can still see his beautiful smile and hear him speak in a way that was so comforting.

Ann MacMillan
UNT Instrument Repair and Instruction

International Trumpet Symposium in Truro, Cornwall, 2006. *Front, left to right*: Helen Sanger, Leigh Anne Hunsaker, Alison Jackson, and Paul Thomas. *Back, left to right*: Randy Tinnin, Jon Cresci, Eric Swisher, Trevor Skinner, Michael Laird, and Keith Johnson.
Courtesy of Leigh Anne Hunsaker.

Keith Johnson and Nathan Little.
Courtesy of Donald Little.

I knew of Keith Johnson long before I met him. Of course, I had read his book and heard of his "greatness" as a University of North Texas professor well before I ever played a note for him. I made the decision to visit UNT in Fall 1999, and it is easily the best decision I ever made regarding my growth as a musician, teacher, and citizen.

I remember fondly how he met me on a Saturday to hear me play and audition for his graduate studio. All the typical "Keith Johnson" mannerisms were there: Very encouraging, gentlemanly, groomed to the tee, and every word that he spoke was pure gold! In casual conversation it seemed as though he had pre-written everything he said.

Like so many others, I felt as though I was suddenly included in some "inner-circle" of trumpet knowledge. Every point was spot on, every comment was impactful and meaningful, and every criticism was constructive. I discovered over the course of five years that I could expect that kind of experience every time I had contact with him, whether I was in a weekly lesson, or in a car on our way to a job, or eating his favorite "comfort food" of fried oysters at a downtown Dallas seafood haunt. He was always passing on wisdom, always leading by example, and always doing the right thing.

So much of how I conduct myself is a direct result of my time with him. He showed me respect, he showed me how to respect others. He was my teacher and always will be. I have never been prouder than to be included in the pantheon of Keith Johnson students. To say he was a great teacher is of course true, but those of us who were his students and colleagues know that he was so much more! He was a great human being who just happened to be one of the best trumpet pedagogues ever!

Thank you, Keith, for everything you shared.

Scott Meredith, Principal Trumpet
Wyoming and Port Angeles Symphonies

I came to North Texas in Fall 1996 to pursue my DMA with Keith. I already had many professional performing and teaching experiences, and I was exceptionally eager to learn everything I could from him in the short residency time of a doctoral program. I can certainly say he helped me immensely in so many areas of my trumpet playing and teaching, but his modeling and mentorship extended far beyond that.

To this day, he defines what it means to be a true gentleman in the music profession. Every day I try to model that same behavior with students and colleagues, and hope I come close to his elegant example.

Rob Murray
Columbus State University

During my second year as a college teacher, I was having a tremendously rough time with some of my colleagues. I spoke with Keith weekly for several months. In hindsight, the fact that he took this time to advise me, since he had a full studio of DMA students, is remarkable. I vividly remember telling him how much I wanted to tell off several people. He laughed, then told me not to let my emotions get the best of me, because that would be what those folks expected. Instead, he suggested I put on my "best shirt and tie," go to work every day, and remember that I was there for my students. I did exactly that, every single day for the next year and continue to do so. I constantly remember his words every time I am dealing with someone who is angry.

Choosing UNT and Keith was the best decision I ever made in my life. He was my musical father, and I trace all the wonderful things I have in my personal and professional life back to Keith. I will love that man until the day I die.

Marc Reed
University of Akron

I remember one day Keith told me that his trumpet had taken him to places he never thought he would go. Today, I can unequivocally say the same thing about my own life and career. When I think about that, it brings a smile to my face. Thank you, Keith!

Susan Rider
"The President's Own" United States Marine Band

My first lesson with Keith Johnson was on the morning of September 11, 2001. Like many other Americans, I watched the news in horror that morning.

I called Keith and asked if we were still having a lesson considering what was taking place in New York. He replied, "Yes, we need to continue our normal lives and not let the terrorists win." I went to my lesson and we just talked. I don't remember playing anything at all. Before the end of my lesson, Professor Brian Bowman knocked on the door and said that school had been cancelled and to go home. I reference this memory because even though it was a tragic day, it showed what kind of man and teacher Keith was. He displayed strength and firm resolution that in turn helped me get through that horrible day. Keith led by example, and I will forever be influenced by my memories of his great intellect, kindness, and strength of character.

Raquel Samayoa
University of North Texas

By the end of my doctoral program, I considered Keith and Cecile close friends. My girlfriend (now wife of nine years) and I joined the Episcopal church that Keith and Cecile attended. My wife Betsy still talks about the time Keith took us to Mr. Chopsticks near campus for lunch one day. She enjoyed the lunch, but still says to this day that she felt like she was meeting my dad. Because my father was in France, I think he wanted to make sure that Betsy was the right fit! Keith attended our wedding along with Dr. Deanna Bush, another UNT music professor. I can still see them laughing at our reception while they drank wine and enjoyed the jazz band. It's a cherished memory I'll carry with me.

Keith Johnson was kind and professional, demanding and understanding, innovative and traditional. He found a balance that not many achieve in their lifetime. I am grateful beyond words for the education I received while studying trumpet with him. I came to UNT to study trumpet, but I left as a better human as well. I often find myself asking the question, "What would Keith do?"

Etienne Stoupy
Acadiana Symphony Orchestra

Time spent with Keith has been one of the delights of my musical life. Whether at his Denton home, where he and Cecile graciously hosted me many times, visiting with him at the New Hampshire Music Festival, or playing together in Texas and California, Keith's gentlemanly calm and engaging presence were always welcome.

In lengthy conversations over dinner and South African red wines, discussing articles in the New York Times *and* Wall Street Journal, *the finer points of Episcopalian liturgy, and the absurdities of politics, it was the inevitable turn to Keith's love of and devotion to his family, his deep faith, dedication to teaching and performing, self-deprecation and ribald sense of humor that touched me most. That, and his serious addiction to Hook, Line and Sinker's deep-fried oysters.*

John Thiessen
Philharmonia Baroque Orchestra

Keith's strength as a teacher went far beyond his ability to make a student play better. Not only did he know what we all needed to hear to be better trumpet players, but also what each person needed to face to defeat their individual demons. He could build you as a person—your inner strength, humility, and love for what you do. That transcendence is what makes him great, and I'm so thankful to have had him as a mentor and teacher in my life.

Ward Yager
U.S. Army Field Band

Surely such chances are not chance,
But encounter always intended.

Afterword

As an undergraduate music education major, I was warned by older students that very little covered in professional education courses was relevant to teaching music. My first day in Principles of Education, we found ten "Truisms of Teaching" on the board and were told to memorize them because they would be on the test. It's probably fair to say that many of us rolled our eyes while dutifully copying the list. The first was: "Teaching is a human relations activity." I don't remember the other nine, but several years later I met a man who exemplified this principle to a degree I had never imagined.

My trumpet lessons at UNT were always the high point of my week, and most of my notes began, "I had a good lesson with Mr. Johnson today." My indelible memory of that first semester is of Keith leaning back in his chair, very relaxed, coffee cup in hand, saying, "You know, playing the trumpet is really very easy." I would doubtfully eye the tangle of notes in my Charlier etude or the Sachse book lurking behind it and think, "Maybe it's easy for you, buddy."

Over the years, his adages worked their way into my playing and into my psyche, and I found that I had learned much from him beyond playing the trumpet. A prolific author and eloquent speaker, he nonetheless taught the most important life lessons by example. He embodied the concept of "music as metaphor" and has become the touchstone for an artist teacher. Keith Johnson is the person whom I would most like to emulate in my personal and professional life.

While preparing this book, I was given access to Keith's home and office files. There I found many photographs, cards, and letters from students dating back to his Iowa years. As a teacher who has kept every card, coffee cup, and pencil holder received from my former students, I realized how special these letters were to him. In more than one conversation over the years, I had tried to tell Keith how much I appreciated all he had done for me, but after seeing these carefully saved mementos, I greatly regretted not having put mine in writing. This book is my thank you note, and I'm grateful I was able to share a preliminary copy with him on Christmas Eve in 2019.

Collecting these stories and tributes has been a vivid reminder of my own student days and has broadened my understanding of Keith Johnson's success in his studio. He once told me that he could sum up his work with Cichowicz and all his other experiences in one word: "Gratitude." I was momentarily surprised but thought I understood what he meant. Today, I believe that I know exactly what he meant, and I feel the same way about my experience with him. If you are fortunate enough to have a person like Keith Johnson in your life, you are blessed indeed.

Leigh Anne Hunsaker

Part Four

ITG Journal Articles

Teaching the Art
of Listening

* This article was based on a lecture/demonstration presented to the
Central Midwest Theory Society Annual Conference, May 4, 1981,
University of Northern Iowa. It appeared in the ITG *Journal*
(October 1981). Reprinted by permission.

Learning to listen well, with thoroughness and objectivity, is the single most important skill any musician must acquire. All other skills are secondary to and dependent upon this primary musical ability.

Music, as an aural art, must never be reduced to the merely theoretical, whether as music theory taught in the classroom, or as the theories of various physical aspects of sound production such as are presented in studio teaching. Leonardo da Vinci said it rather well, although he was referring, of course, to the visual arts: "Theory must never be allowed to outstrip practice."

I do not wish to tell you how to go about teaching your classes in music theory, and I would not presume to intrude upon your specific area of professional expertise. I would be so presumptuous, however, as to suggest what you should be teaching, since I firmly believe the primary purpose of your work in the classroom and mine in the studio are one and the same – the creation of better musicians.

Quite a few years ago when I was a college student, I had the misfortune to study with a music theory teacher who managed to teach theory as if it were some mathematical formula, devoid of all expression, variety, or interest. Every aspect, whether in part writing, ear training, or form was reduced to a rule or a predictable pattern. Examinations in listening were particular occasions of genuine fear, and frequently I saw mature, healthy and talented individuals literally driven to tears.

I recently completed work on a book about various aspects of trumpet performance, and in the course of my research I had occasion to do fairly extensive readings in such areas as learning theories, motivation, and environmental influences. One of the things I learned beyond any doubt, at least in my mind, is that the atmosphere and conditions in which an idea is presented are as crucial to the absorption and utilization of that idea as is the intrinsic merit of the idea itself. There is an excellent book on performance skills, any performance skills really, written in laymen's terms and highly readable. It is titled *The Inner Game of Tennis*, and I have found it to be one of the most helpful books on performance available today. I would also suggest that it might be of value to anyone involved in teaching or learning the art of listening.

As an applied teacher, I came relatively late in life to a realization of how critical fine, accurate listening is to my success, in terms of my own performance as well as in teaching my students. Part of this late development may be rightly attributed to innate slowness on my part, but at least some of the blame must rest on the teacher to whom I referred earlier. He failed in what I consider to be our primary purpose – the enhancement of our students' musicianship.

My applied teaching was, for some years, highly analytical in a physiological sense. I took considerable pride in being able to discuss the functions of the orbicularis oris as opposed to the buccinator or to state boldly, and correctly, that the diaphragm is not, in strictest medical terms, a muscle. (For those concerned with such matters, it is a musculo-fibrous membrane.) What I came to discover was that all this technical information did not

make me a better performer, and while it may have made me a more interesting teacher (trumpet players are notoriously fascinated with their own
physiognomy, a kind of musical narcissism) – I doubt that such information
really made me a better teacher.

About this time two especially pertinent things happened to me. First,
I began working with a teacher of great humaneness, erudition, and, above
all, musicianship. He had me do such things as sing my etudes and play
melodies just on the mouthpiece, and perhaps most importantly he played for
me a great deal. The more I studied with him the more my playing improved,
and yet when I tried to analyze what he had instructed me to do, there was
no answer that satisfactorily accounted for the changes in my performance.
Hi usual comments were something like, "Relax, take a full breath and sing."
Hardly revelatory statements! – but finally it dawned on me what he had
taught me – sound, musicianship, and above all, the necessity of listening
really well. He had forced me in his kind way to hear the differences between
our sounds, and once I started to hear those differences I began, more uncon-
sciously than consciously, to alter physical responses far more effectively
than I had by extensive, detailed physical analyses of my playing.

About this same time I began, through a variety of circumstances, to
become more involved in recording sessions. For anyone who has done
any serious work in recordings, the early revelations are strong and often
shattering. We do not, unfortunately, usually listen very objectively until
we are forced to do so by that infernal machine, the tape recorder. The tape
recorder failed to recognize that I had been a good student at large trumpet
schools or that I had studied for many years with several well-known
trumpet teachers. It hardly even cared when my new daughter kept me
up most of the night before a recording session or that my boss had upset
me with a dirty look that morning because my long-distance phone bill at
school was outrageously high.

The machine did tell me the truth, however, and, even more importantly,
it taught me to hear the truth, at least partially. And that, of course, is the
beginning of learning to listen.

Now many of you are no doubt saying to yourself at this point – "Does
this person think he is actually revealing something new to us? Does he really

think his experience is so unique?" Well, my answer is a strong no, I do not believe my experience was unique, and that is precisely my point. I was a conscientious student in two of the best music schools in this country, and yet I managed to end up with little appreciation of how desperately I needed first to learn to listen before I could develop as a musician.

When a little child begins the process of learning to speak he makes all the phonetic sounds possible before eventually sorting out those which have meaning and which he hears frequently in his environment. Children who speak such different languages as German, Swahili, Urdu, and English all make the same sounds at first. When certain sounds obtain certain responses for the child, those sounds are retained, reutilized, and, with practice, perfected. Wise parents patiently and clearly repeat sounds as often as necessary until the child, through the selective process we call trial and error, is able to imitate what he hears. The two critical factors in this process are first that the child hear the correct sounds as often as necessary and secondly that he practice reproducing those sounds in an atmosphere of patience, thoroughness, and encouragement. Even mistakes are not to be discouraged, because they are a necessary component of the sorting out process.

It is easy to imagine the trauma which would beset an infant if his first faulty efforts at speech were met with the same kind of criticism which await most music students' early efforts. And here I lay greatest blame on the private instructor who attributes a bad sound immediately to a faulty motor response such as poor embouchure formation or awkward hand position rather than the student's having inadequately heard the desired sound clearly before attempting to reproduce it.

The ultimate goal of all music instruction should, in my opinion, be improved musical performance, and I do not mean just from the players' perspective. Listeners who are informed and critical (in the best sense of the term) are as essential to performance as the players. Whether we are teaching classes in music theory, giving private applied instruction or doing research in some relatively remote aspect of historical musicology, we should ultimately have as our goal improvement in the final musical product, which both instigated our endeavors and to which their eventual consummation is directed. Our efforts may be toward a better understanding of the formal construction of a work, greater technical facility of a particular part, or an historically more authentic performance. Whatever our specific contribution, it should ultimately result in improvement in the actual musical product created.

I spend quite a bit of time each year performing and giving workshops for public school students. During these visits I am repeatedly struck by what I perceive to be the most obvious deficiency in both students and music teachers – the lack of genuine musicianship.

During a workshop last fall, a band director I was visiting, unaware of the extent of my failings as a conductor, asked me to rehearse his band. I picked from his folder a Mozart overture, one which I have played many times, and one which presents no meter changes, thinking, "at least I won't get lost waving my hands." The arranger who scored this work for band had, in a state of semi-enlightenment decided to add a snare drum for the entire length of the piece. (In his defense I must say that it is customary, in fact virtually mandatory, in school editions to keep everyone in the band busy, particularly the drummers, a section often known more for their gamesmanship than their musicianship.) After about four bars of trying to hear the overture through the din of half a dozen snare drums I stopped, pointed out to the director that I thought perhaps historical considerations indicated the deletion of the snare drums, and went on. (Never mind the even larger question of whether a high school band should be playing the overture to a Mozart opera at all.) The director was quite impressed with the improvement. I am happy to report the director in this instance was a graduate of another large music school in Iowa, not, unfortunately, that our graduates or probably those of most schools are exempt from such failings.

The point is that the director, while highly organized and successful in many categories by which music teachers are judged, was seriously weak in musicianship. His listening was so poor that he was not even bothered by the totally inappropriate use of percussion.

This example may seem a bit extreme, but it is really not all that exceptional. And in terms of the problems of students, the effect of poor listening skills is even greater.

Several years ago I was giving a workshop for band directors. Near the close of the session one of the directors posed an interesting question to me. "What," he said, "is the most pervasive weakness you notice in entering college trumpet students?" Answers which he might have expected would, I suspect, have included improper respiratory function, range, embouchure, or any of several other technical matters. Instead I simply said, "Students do not know how to listen well."

My students come to school more often than not with technical abilities which far exceed their musical development. When I give high school workshops I always ask if there are students in the group who participate in athletics. Inevitably there seem to be tennis players and basketball players (most other sports apparently present more conflicts with band). When I ask the students what famous performers they like most to watch in their chosen sport I get a fairly long and impressive recitation of names. When I then ask the same students what professional players they most prefer to listen to on their respective instruments I am almost always met with a blank ex pression. Somehow it never dawns on them, and even more sadly, they are rarely taught, that in order to play music one must first know how music sounds. I ask them if they can imagine learning the rules of rugby or soccer and immediately going into a game without ever having seen a game played. Impossible, of course, and ultimately as boring, frustrating and defeating as trying to play Mozart without knowing how Mozart can sound.

If I may use as an example a specific problem relating to trumpet playing, I would like to try to show you how the conceptions of a certain sound alter physical response. But first, let me give you a little illustration of the stimulus/response approach to teaching patterns of physical behavior. The idea is simply to alter the response by altering the stimulus. Imagine that I pitched a simple object, such as a pencil, to someone, first to their right side, then to their left side. The person's neuromuscular system is so sophisticated that without consciously thinking he will alter the psychomotor responses and catch the pencil as it is pitched first to one side and then the other. The solution to catching the pencil is not to alter responses by changing conscious verbal instructions, that is, consciously telling oneself to move one's hands in a given direction, but to alter responses by changing perceptions.

Now, what happens when a person attempts to create musical sounds? We must, of course, allow for a lengthy sorting out period, the kind we referred to earlier that a child goes through learning to speak. But throughout all our attempts to create music we must constantly keep uppermost in our minds the sounds we wish to hear and eventually play. Learning to hear a sound before we play, what is sometimes referred to as pre-hearing and is sometimes called audiation, is the best source of direction for any physical responses. Suppose I say a certain simple sound for you. To reproduce or imitate this sound you would not go through a long technical analysis of the many physiological and kinesiological responses necessary to recreate that sound. Your mind and body are such an incredible instrument that, even if you are not a trained singer, you can reproduce approximately the sound I sang.

Consider for a moment another situation, this time a more technical problem in which listening can be used to guide the physical implementation of a very complex behavioral response – breathing. I teach students respiratory function by having them first say for me the sound OH. Then HO. Then, I have them breathe in and out very relaxed and very deeply making the sounds OH and HO, with the breath, listening to the sound very critically. It must be exactly what one wants. If the sounds are good the breath meets all the tests which can be applied, tests of fullness, smoothness, openness and, ultimately, velocity and flexibility.

Now obviously, what I have just shown you is a very specific, limited example of how good listening can be used to implement technical responses. You, as experienced teachers and performers, must extend such a theory to your own realm of expertise. What is most critical to remember is that inherent in any musical sound are the necessary instructions for the reproduction of that sound, depending on the ability of the musician to hear first the musical idea completely and secondly to process and use the physical responses necessary for its implementation. In one of the graduate courses I teach I present several lectures on various styles of orchestral brass playing. I ask the students to identify a number of different world class orchestras by the sound of their brass sections. At first the students are a bit intimidated, but they rather soon take to it, and their listening skills improve by leaps and bounds. No serious singer is likely to confuse Gerard Souzay with Dietrich

Fischer-Dieskau, and no pianist would mistake Vladimir Horowitz's playing for that of Alfred Brendel's.

The point is that we must use whatever means we can conceive to teach students to listen well. In my lessons I have my students sing, so much so that my students must think sometimes that I am a frustrated singer. I am! I have them play etudes by buzzing the mouthpiece. I have them bring me lists of recordings they have listened to since the previous lesson, and they must be prepared to discuss in excruciating detail what they heard – what, for example, is unusual about the tone quality of the first oboe in the Berlin Philharmonic? Does Glenn Gould use any pedal when he plays Bach? What national school of clarinet playing uses large amounts of vibrato? And so on.

If you will permit me a simplistic analogy, I would like to draw a comparison between a musician and a fine stereo system. The speakers are the outlet for the sound, much like an instrument. The amplification or energy system could be compared to the breath of a wind player, the bow of the string player, and so on. But what ultimately makes or breaks the system is the source of the sound, the record. No matter what the quality of the production system (or more accurately, the reproduction system) the source of the sound is the chief determinant of the quality of music eventually produced. Whether a violinist, composer, or our aforementioned snare drummer, the musician's mind and the sounds he hears and creates therein, are the critical issues.

It is not enough to hear pitch, though heaven knows this would represent an improvement in many cases. We must create more erudite, imaginative, critical and above all, musical listeners. The methods of doing this in the studio may differ from those in the classroom. But whether we are in the studio, theory class, band, orchestra rehearsal, or music history section, our primary efforts must be directed at creating better musicians, and the first and continually most important step in that undertaking is to rigorously, patiently and as thoroughly as possible, teach the art of listening.

Good Respiratory Practices for Brass Performers

This article was originally presented as a clinic at the Texas Music Educators Association Convention in San Antonio on February 11, 1988. It appeared in the *ITG Journal* (May 1990). Reprinted by permission.

I use two criteria by which to judge the usefulness of information and ideas I present to my students or use in my clinics. Because we should deal only with information that has merit, the first criterion is obvious: Is the information correct? Does it make sense and seem reasonable? The second criterion is of equal importance: Can the ideas under consideration be presented in a simple, direct manner that will make them of value to the player in improving performance? If an idea must be expressed in a complex form that cannot readily be used by the player under the stress of performance, then it is of no use. What I am presenting has been chosen in light of these two premises.

Before I give suggestions concerning how to improve breathing habits, I would like to discuss several basic respiratory conditions in a broad and general way.

When taking even the simplest breath, two groups of muscles are involved: those of inhalation and those of exhalation. It is important to understand the difference between positive muscular effort (in this case inhaling air or blowing it out) and isometric tension; that is, muscle working against muscle. Each of the two major muscle groups of inhalation and exhalation works best when working positively without opposition from the other. What is sometimes referred to as control or support is often really a misplaced attempt to govern the action of one set of muscular responses by setting in action an opposite muscular force. This creates what Edward Tarr refers to in the *New Grove Dictionary* (Vol. 19, p. 222) as the "hard belly" school of wind playing rather than the more relaxed approach that is really positive respiratory effort. This isometric tension often misleads the wind player, because it makes him feel as if he is working very hard and, therefore, must be doing the right thing.

What we should be seeking in proper breathing is motion, not isometric tension or a sense of support. "Good" air is always moving. It is either moving in or it is moving out. If it is static, it is "bad" air and will almost certainly lead to an increase in tension and a restricted sound.

Consider for a moment the difference between air flow and compression. Air flow refers to the speed with which the air moves in or out. Compression refers to the pressure of the air stream. Certain instruments, such as the tuba, utilize enormous rates of air flow, but that air is under a very low rate of compression. The oboe and the trumpet in the upper register actually have quite low flow level, but such breath frequently attains high levels of compression. In my opinion, the flow rate should always be as high as possible for the pitch frequency and dynamic level sought. This property of motion in the breath produces a higher degree of efficiency in tone production and results in a warmer, freer quality of sound. Keep in mind that as a player changes registers the flow rate/compression level relationship changes. As a player goes lower the flow rate increases and compression is lowered. The reverse occurs, of course, as he ascends.

Another important condition concerns how efficiently and effectively we coordinate and direct the physical behavior necessary to any willful creative act, whether playing a brass instrument or swinging a golf club. The portion of the brain which best controls specific neuro-muscular responses is called the subconscious mind. The conscious mind conceives the idea. The subconscious mind, which is actually the more sophisticated, directs the particular neuro-muscular responses necessary to implement that act. As I think Arnold Jacobs might state it, our job is to concentrate on the sound we want to produce, and let the sub-conscious mind take care of the means of production.

For example, take the way we all learned to speak as children. When you first attempted to speak, at the age of a year or so, your parents pronounced "Mommy" or "Daddy" for you over and over. Your initial efforts to reproduce this sound were probably less than totally satisfactory, but your parents wisely persisted by repeatedly providing for you a model of sound. They pronounced the word(s) for you again and again and allowed you the freedom to experiment with various sounds until the one you produced matched (more or less) the concept they provided you. Fortunately, they did not, at the first poor attempt you made to pronounce a simple word, ship you off to a speech therapist who tried to "fix" your incorrect speech by telling you exactly "how" to breathe, how far apart to place your teeth, or what the exact position of the lips or teeth or tongue should be. You were allowed to improve by repeated attempts to speak the word in question without any consciousness of the specific physical behaviors involved in such speech.

You learned by imitation, which involves repeated patterns of stimulus and response. It is my strong contention that this is the most natural, significant way we learn, and it seems highly appropriate to me for learning most, perhaps all, of the various aspects of playing an instrument.

In the case of wind instruments, the stimuli should take the form of sounds whenever possible. Long, elaborate verbal instructions, however correct, violate the premise concerning the need for good ideas to be presented in a simple, usable form. They also do not approach the learning of performance skills or the natural process we follow when learning to speak, sing, dance, or play a sport.

We do not control muscular behavior as well when we try to think directly of the muscles involved as we do when we think of some stimulus or concept that, with practice, will trigger the proper responses. In other words, to get a certain kind of sound, we must first think that sound.

The body only does what the mind tells it to do. Therefore, to provide the best set of instructions for the mind, it is necessary to think clearly of the sound we want to produce. Our conscious mind should focus on the sound, that is, the end product, and leave the implementation of that sound to the subconscious mind which controls particular muscular responses to a much greater degree of refinement and sophistication.

Think sound, not feeling and judge sound, not feeling. After playing a passage or piece, my students often remark, "That felt terrible" or "That really felt good." My response, often to their dismay, is that it doesn't matter how it felt. What matters is "How did it sound?" No conductor or member of an audience cares how you feel when you play; they only care how you sound. They are correct. The truth is that judging performance by sound rather than by feeling is much more accurate and stimulates better and more consistent physical responses. One day you may feel fresh, the next day tired, the next day nervous, and so on. Feelings are often misleading, but the sound is objective. By using sound to guide your playing the specific adjustments that must be made to achieve your playing goals can be accomplished as a response to the concept of sound that directs your playing.

Here are some specific suggestions as to how to improve your breathing. First, let us consider the importance of posture. When I was a boy my mother would admonish me to sit or stand up straight and not to slouch. I gave very little thought to her advice until many years later when I went to Chicago for a lesson with Arnold Jacobs. When he asked me what in particular about my playing was concerning me, I responded that I would really like to work with him on breathing. He said, not too gently, "A big guy like you? Why, there's nothing wrong with your breathing except you are lazy. Sit up straight and take a big breath!"

Good posture is such an obvious condition for good respiratory function that it is almost always taken for granted and often abused or neglected.

Good posture is absolutely essential for good breathing, and fortunately, it is extremely easy to achieve. The only difficult part is remembering to use it.

First, stand (or sit) tall. Reach upward with the crown of the head so that the spine reaches a position of gentle elongation. The upper part of the thorax should be moderately elevated (not exaggerated) and the shoulders should hang naturally and free of tension. The overall condition should be comfortable and relaxed, yet alert and responsive. There should be no tension anywhere. Remember that what we should be seeking is a breath characterized by full, free motion, not tense muscular contraction.

After years of reading about approaches to teaching breathing and listening to many players speak about the subject, I have reached the conclusion that the best way to achieve good respiratory habits is not by seeking to acquire an abundance of technical knowledge about the breathing process, but to concentrate directly on making the sound of a good breath. By using the vowel sounds OH or AH, one can breathe in and out a full, flowing air column that can be readily adjusted to accommodate pitch level or dynamics as warranted by the music.

Making the proper sound by using these single syllables will trigger virtually all the physical responses required for a good breath, and these sounds certainly meet the requirements of effectiveness and simplicity of use. They are easy to produce, easy to remember, and they work!

When dealing with most aspects of performance, it is better to employ general, broad concepts rather than narrow, specific ones. Concentrate on the end, not the means. By thinking of the sound of a good breath rather than trying consciously to think of the mechanical intricacies of respiration, we take and use better breaths, and that is our objective. We need to learn that we play best when we think creatively rather than analytically.

A crucial factor in the effectiveness of our breathing is the volume of air we inhale. A reasonably full breath makes playing easier and produces a more beautiful sound than a small breath. In part, the ease with which the air is expelled is determined by the total amount of air we take, and the out-flow of the breath is much more efficient when the inhalation is volu minous.

For purposes of wind playing, the upper one-half to two-thirds of our air supply comes out most efficiently. If one has a vital capacity of six liters of air, this gives the player a good sounding air supply of three or four liters of efficient air. When we use our lower reserves we must work much harder to expel the air, and the sound quality reflects this extra labor. Each time we breathe we should take a full breath, use that breath as freely as possible, and then refill fully. We always should seek to breathe fully and use up the air. One might visualize this as a string player using the bow fully, from frog to tip. Few phrases require that we expel all our air, but we should use the breath as freely as possible. Get rid of stale, excess air when appropriate, and start again with a full, fresh breath.

Consider briefly two specific situations relating to the breath, because they seem to be problems which most younger players encounter as they develop their playing technique. The first situation concerns the kind of room in which most people practice. Frequently, we practice in a small area such as a bedroom or practice cubicle. Such rooms are much smaller than the places where we actually perform, and this can mislead one into reducing the "size" of the sound and the amount of air necessary in a real concert hall. I am not referring exclusively to dynamic level, but to an over-all approach to the fullness and depth of sound. Most small rooms need to be overplayed in order for the player to adequately develop the kinds of sources and dynamic range necessary for large halls. One must imagine the kind of space where the actual performance will occur, and practice accordingly.

The second consideration relates to one's approach to soft playing. Frequently players interpret soft dynamic markings as a kind of negative dynamic, as if a soft passage were really a loud passage held back. What happens in this instance is that a high level of blowing effort is maintained, but isometric tension is employed to reduce the dynamic level. The result-ing sound is characterized by tightness and instability. An analogy would be trying to regulate the speed of an automobile by pressing the accelerator all the way down and controlling the speed with the brake pedal. It is much better to blow freely with positive energy at a level appropriate to the pitch and dy namics. Blowing air should always be positive, not negative.

Consider some specific exercises that will help develop a full, free flowing approach to breathing. Work with the vowel sounds OH for inha-lation and HO for exhalation. For the first exercise, use a metronome set at quarter-note = 60. Using a four-count measure, breathe in on the fourth count, breathe out on counts one and two, and rest on count three. Allow the breath to be exhaled as freely as possible.

Remember to take a "fill-up" fully and to empty the breath as quickly and freely as possible. There should be no delay between inhaling and exhaling. Any delay between breathing in and breathing out will almost certainly introduce unwanted tension into the process. The air should always be flowing in or flowing out; it should never be static. The same general procedure may be followed at various faster and slower speeds in order to practice moving the air more rapidly or more gently as would be required at different volume and/or pitch levels.

We may, for example, practice the same exercise at a tempo of quarter-note = 40, which might replicate the air speed of a much softer passage. However, no inference should be drawn that one should always inhale for one full beat before commencing exhalation. Rather than trying to quantitatively define the amount of time necessary for every breath, I prefer to encourage players to think of the inhalation as being in the character of the passage to be played. The air should be inspired in a velocity commensurate with the style of expiration. The inhalation to play a loud fast passage, a Sousa march, for example, would be taken more vigorously and rapidly than a breath to play the soft opening trumpet passage to *Rienzi*. The way the air is to be blown out should determine the way the air is taken in. The inhalation and exhalation are really the same air, merely traveling in opposite directions. The best guidance we can provide for our physical responses comes from thinking of the musical sounds we wish to produce!

Some players, usually because of long-standing habits, have difficulty relaxing enough to implement the OH or AH vowel sound. The throat may be tight and the thorax and/or abdominal area tense. There are a couple of useful devices such players may find helpful in practicing a more open, relaxed approach to breathing.

One of the simplest, cheapest, most available and effective tools to help correct poor breathing is a simple tube, a few inches long. A tube such as a plastic pipe fitting, 3/4" in diameter (available at any hardware store for less than one dollar) can help any player whose respiration is shallow or tense. Simply insert the tube into the mouth an inch or so and breathe in and out through the tube energetically; It is virtually impossible to introduce tension into the respiratory system when using such a device. By breathing in and out vigorously through the tube the player will hear clearly the kind of sound to the breath which we are seeking. This sound can then be imitated without the tube. I recommend using only the 3/4" diameter tube. Anything narrower is restrictive of air flow. Anything larger tends to force the front of the mouth open too wide and the back part of the hinged jaw too closed, thus creating tension.

Another useful device for helping players develop a sense of voluminous respiration is a rubber air bag which can be found in medical supply stores. The most common size is the five-liter bag. Having a student take a vigorous breath and then blow into the bag encourages the practice of using large volumes of air in inspiration and expiration. Most players I have observed simply use too small an amount of air. This causes inefficiency and poorer sound quality than might otherwise be achieved.

Another way to help a player breathe more freely and fully is to tell the player to draw the breath into the mouth as if he had just taken a bite of very hot food and wanted to draw air across his tongue to cool it off. My students refer to this as a "pizza breath," because I often tell them to breathe as if they had just eaten a piece of extremely hot pizza. This has the effect of lowering the tongue within the oral cavity and allows the air to flow in with less resistance. Whenever tension occurs within the respiratory system the tongue tends to rise, partially restricting the air flow. The tongue should be equally unobtrusive during exhalation.

In order to ensure that the air moves quickly, it is often helpful to ask a player to blow air at a particular object such as one's hand or perhaps a specific point across the room. The player needs to develop the sense that air is blown some distance across the lips rather than merely at the lips. All these exercises should be done at various degrees of velocity and always with positive effort, never tension. Any degree of tension reduces the quality and quantity of the air column.

I strongly recommend that players begin each day's practice with a minute or two of work on one or more of the exercises I have mentioned. The full utilization of our respiratory abilities is a somewhat elusive quality, and if a player does not continually and seriously work to improve his use of the air, a deterioration will inevitably occur. The use of the air will either improve through conscientious practice, or it will worsen through neglect. It will not reach a plateau and simply remain there.

Also, as we age, there is a gradual reduction in our respiratory capabilities. This reduction can be greatly slowed by faithful, vigorous, extensive work on proper breathing.

Finally, let me suggest that one practice extensively on the mouthpiece only or with one of the readily available devices such as the B.E.R.P. Keep in mind a full, free-flowing air column. By playing only the mouthpiece, most players seem to have a better understanding of how well they are or are not using the air. As brass players we must come to terms with the idea that we, not the instrument, are the source of the sound. The instrument, merely amplifies and gives a certain timbre. Like singers, we are the source of the energy supply, the air; and we provide the vibrating membranes (the lips) which respond to that air. The quality and quantity of our air supply have far more to do with our level of success than all the other physical aspects of brass playing combined. Good, relaxed posture and a free, voluminous inhalation followed immediately by a rich, flowing exhalation will make anyone's playing easier, more efficient, and more beautiful to hear.

The University Musician

This article appeared in the *ITG Journal* (May 1994).
Reprinted by permission.

Opportunities

In the United States and Canada and to a lesser extent in many other countries, the responsibility for developing musicians has been taken over by the college and university systems of higher education. Musical training, once perceived as narrow and professional, has now been incorporated into traditional academic settings, complete with an extensive dose of liberal arts/general education curricula. This is not to say that conservatories do not exist; they do, and many of them offer fine training. They tend, however, to emphasize study directed rather exclusively toward professional playing careers, and many young people today (or perhaps, more accurately, the parents of many young people) seek a broader educational program.

The incorporation of the musical training that was once the exclusive domain of conservatories into colleges and universities has produced some notable results, in many instances still maintaining the highest performance standards. The relationship between music programs and other elements of the academy are not always easy or peaceful, however. The creative arts require a certain kind of thinking that is often different (not necessarily better or worse) than more traditional (at least for the academy) intellectual pursuits. This tension that exists between music (also art and drama) and the rest of the campus population is on-going, and at times, troublesome. Most music schools of any real quality have spent considerable time and energy examining their place in and relationship to the rest of the university. Do they emphasize a kind of narrower conservatory focus, do they try to educate the student in a high degree of professional excellence *and* in traditional liberal arts, or do they weigh in on the side of general education, hoping that each student's individual initiative will lead to professional development? These considerations are ongoing at most quality institutions, with the emphasis changing according to the cultural and political climate of the time and the views of those in charge at the moment.

Anyone contemplating a career as a musician in academia should understand these philosophies and tensions. They have an enormous influence on the character of individual schools, and, consequently, on how individual faculty members develop their careers and are rewarded (or not) for their accomplishments.

A young person hoping for a career as a university musician needs to know something of the kinds of settings in which he or she might work, and, when possible, match one's talents to the setting. As a practical matter, college teaching positions are difficult to obtain, and one must often (particularly at the entry level) take whatever is available. In such a situation it is imperative that the new teacher understand not only the particular duties assigned, but the general philosophy or atmosphere in which such duties will be carried out. Great flexibility is needed on the part of the new, untenured instructor.

One of the most attractive features of university music teaching is the potential for the variety which the work offers. While one's particular interest may be in trumpet performance, opportunities usually exist – and often it is a job requirement – to participate in several types of musical endeavors. One will also have to serve on committees, both departmental and interdisciplinary, to do research, lecture, travel, and take an active role in the broader functions of the academy. One of the most stimulating and rewarding features of university life is being a part of a diverse and interesting community of artists and scholars.

Such stimulation must not, however, be allowed to interfere with continued progress in one's special discipline. Such a seduction is an easy and professionally deadly trap. Working in a university, for most musicians, represents a continuous struggle between being an outstanding performer/teacher and taking a full role in the life of the department, college or university. More later about this problem of balancing various aspects of a career.

One of the most compelling reasons for wanting to practice one's musical art in a university setting is the opportunity to work with gifted students. Students who are eager, dedicated, questioning, persistent, and talented provide satisfaction and professional stimulation unequaled by any other source. I often tell my students, not entirely in jest, that the key to being considered a successful teacher is to choose one's students well. Fine students are a real source of joy and sense of reward.

A significant, if sometimes onerous, part of university life is committee work. Universities are run by committees. Participation is expected in most settings. Unfortunately, most committees take an inordinately long time to accomplish little, usually preferring to spend most of their collective energy fighting the last war. When all other life forms on the planet have become extinct, undoubtedly a group of that most protected species, tenured full professors, will still be holding committee meetings, debating subjects arcane, obtuse, and irrelevant. Nevertheless, committees do offer young teachers the opportunity to express ideas, to meet other faculty and in rare cases, to actually influence the direction of education.

Colleges and universities are frequently places that can provide considerable intellectual and artistic resources. Grants, research assistance, released time, and support services are often available free or at very low cost. Aid for professional travel, continued study, and even publication can sometimes be had for the asking. The key to exploiting such possibilities is a willingness to explore, ask questions, and, of course, fill out application forms.

One of the most attractive aspects of being a university musician is the job security most positions afford the faculty member. Any professor who successfully completes the tenure process will in all likelihood be assured a reasonably secure position for life. While the financial rewards are rarely substantial, the knowledge that one's position is permanent becomes more and more attractive in a seemingly less stable economy.

Negative Considerations

There are a number of negative items which any musician contemplating an academic career should consider. There are, unfortunately, relatively few positions compared to the number of people seeking such positions. I have known of trumpet positions for which applications have numbered more than one hundred. While this number may seem lower than those for some orchestral positions, it should be remembered that orchestral positions do not require the attainment of specific degree levels. The ever-increasing number of people holding advanced degrees continues to worsen the relationship between supply and demand. In other disciplines where jobs in the private sector pay much better than academia (business and the sciences come to mind first) departments sometimes have difficulty recruiting any qualified candidates. Not so in music. Some fields (musicology and theory) are even more crowded than applied music.

Because the number of positions in specific musical fields is low, the opportunity to choose an exact location becomes difficult. I occasionally deal with students who wish to locate in a particular area. They quickly learn that being too selective is a sure ticket to unemployment. It is important to remember that the first job is the hardest to get. After that, if one is successful, opportunities become at least a little more abundant.

Perhaps the most serious concern for any accomplished musician considering entering the academic world is the question of salary. In general, salaries for college music teachers are low. On many campuses throughout this country teachers in the arts are the lowest paid faculty members. This sad fact is a reflection of the low priority our culture assigns to fine arts and a simple question of supply and demand: too few physicists and too many trumpet players!

Musicians working in a university setting often think success will come if only their performances and teaching are excellent. While those activities are vital, there is much more. Music professors are frequently judged and their economic progress determined by traditional academics who do not understand that solo and ensemble performance *are* publication. Our efforts are presented in a public forum and juried by virtually every member of the audience. Because of this unfortunate ignorance regarding the nature of our work on the part of the larger community, we must be certain to make our case to administrators and review committees. Otherwise, we and all our talented young colleagues suffer, and, of course, ultimately our students and our art form lose. We must be willing to take an active role in the larger university community, if for no other reason than to explain what we do and how it should be evaluated properly. Such participation is ultimately a matter of survival.

Qualifications

There are a number of ways in which one can go about preparing for a career in university music teaching. More and more, the earned doctorate is mandatory. Needless to say, all degrees should be from high quality, well-respected schools whenever possible (although what one obtains from a degree is dependent more on one's efforts than on a particular school or teacher). A trumpet player who attends a reputable school that has a distinguished teacher may get a closer look by a search committee than an equally good player from an unknown school. I do not argue for or against the rightness of this situation; I only point out its existence.

As mentioned earlier, most entry-level positions require the faculty member to teach in different areas. Combinations such as trumpet/band, trumpet/jazz, trumpet/music education and trumpet/music history or theory are common. In many cases the number of areas in which the faculty member is expected to teach may number as many as half a dozen. One should consider carefully how many different disciplines and preparations can be handled simultaneously. Eventually one's skills (not to mention one's time and energy) become diluted, making advancement to a better position harder.

The Doctor of Musical Arts in trumpet performance is becoming more and more the prevalent terminal degree. The intent seems to be to turn out graduates who present a combination of fine musicianship, pedagogical skills, and solid academic knowledge. In order to obtain an initial position and eventually become tenured, the earned doctorate is clearly the most efficient and accepted means today, and any young person seriously considering a career in a university needs to accept the idea that this route, while not the only possible one, is overwhelmingly the norm.

There are alternatives, however, and though the number of people with such alternate qualifications who are progressing through the ranks of college teaching is decreasing, such approaches may still be an option for a select few.

With the wide-spread acceptance of the DMA in performance as the standard terminal degree, it is more than a little ironic that most of the best-known teachers, in fact, hold no doctorate. A further irony is that many schools of lesser quality *insist* on their faculty holding doctorates from the top schools that place minimal emphasis on the degrees of their own faculty. Rather, the finest schools take a more liberal approach and look for performance and teaching accomplishments, minimizing the concern for specific degrees.

What this means for the young performer is that if one is truly outstanding *and* more than a little lucky, there is the slight possibility of obtaining a position and progressing through a career without a doctorate.

Generally, anyone hired at a top-tier school is a person with an established reputation as a player/teacher, and a young player may not be well served by taking such a route. Times and expectations are clearly changing, and this avenue is a most difficult one.

The young person should be advised to view the non- doctorate approach as unconventional. Since, in most cases, the schools that place little emphasis on degrees are among the finest we have, they seldom represent the entry-level positions for which young players are likely to be considered.

Getting the Job

A number of specific steps must be followed in order to obtain a position in higher education. First, one must be aware of the sources that list vacancies. *The Chronicle of Higher Education*, the College Music Society, the International Trumpet Guild, and placement offices of member National Association of Schools of Music (NASM) should all be checked regularly. Notices should be read carefully, and all instructions regarding materials and deadlines should be scrupulously followed.

The process begins with the candidate's letter of application, accompanied by whatever additional materials have been requested. The opening letter should be brief and to the point. Tell who you are and give your present situation. Mention that you are including whatever information has been asked for (resume, letters of reference, tapes, etc.). Supply *only* what is requested. Do not send tapes unless/until asked. Make certain that persons writing on your behalf do so in a timely fashion.

All correspondence should be as well written as possible. Poor grammar, spelling, or syntax are simply unacceptable in a university application. I have known of candidates whose application got no further than the initial letter because of writing errors.

Today a high-quality tape recording is a necessity. Unfortunately, such a tape can be costly to produce, but it is essential in today's competitive market. One must be willing to spend serious time and money to produce a product that will stand up to that submitted by other applicants.

If no specific material is called for, produce a tape of 20 minutes to an hour in duration. Avoid making a tape that is entirely standard fare. My experience has been that lesser known works will often get a more attentive hearing. Likewise, when one gets to the live audition, a piece not already heard many times might get the committee's attention better than yet another performance of an already overplayed standard piece.

Most young persons have little experience with the interview/audition process most positions require. Ask your teacher to practice with you in a mock interview as well as listen to your audition material. Committees are looking for excellent musicians who can present themselves well in a public situation. Clear thinking, poise, and articulate, honest expression are highly valued. Committees are looking for highly competent, enthusiastic people who know how to work in a collegial manner.

Doing the Job

I would make a number of general suggestions to any young college music teacher. First, if one has more than one job offer, seek a position that seems to offer professional flexibility and opportunity for personal and musical growth. If senior colleagues are still productive and secure, the young faculty member can at least hope for good support and guidance. If senior faculty are burned out, embittered, or unenthusiastic, the work environment is likely to be at best mediocre, and at worst, hostile. Older faculty who are insecure and easily threatened can make life miserable for young faculty.

Look for schools that have enlightened, progressive administrators who will support and encourage new faculty. Make certain you know the expectations for your work, and stay in touch with administrators and senior faculty who will be involved in your evaluations.

Approach any job as if you will be there for a lifetime. Work congenially, seeking to build relationships as well as specific programs. Whether one stays a long time in one place or moves soon, looking at any position as permanent will influence you to work in a more positive manner. One of my teachers once gave me some great advice by suggesting that one may either keep changing positions in hopes of finding the ideal job or work to make the job you are in an ideal one. The latter approach is certainly the more productive.

The specific requirements of most trumpet positions are obvious: playing, teaching, and recruiting are usually paramount. Other, somewhat more tangential, duties may include committee work, more traditional forms of publication, and occasionally even fund-raising. The important thing is to do as well as possible in all one's responsibilities, but to always remember to keep priorities straight. I know too many trumpet teachers who long ago allowed their playing to lapse, causing irreparable damage to their credibility.

Progressing through the academic ranks is important for several reasons. First, there is usually some monetary reward attached to promotion. Second, academic advancement is a sign that colleagues recognize one's accomplishments. While one might argue that the monetary rewards of teaching are so slight and the system of hoops one must jump through to achieve promotion are more political than substantive, in some instances the system does work as intended. Guidelines for promotion and tenure should be clearly defined, and, if properly conceived and administered, should guide the younger faculty member to a more productive career.

Perhaps the greatest challenge in any career is to be able to practice one's profession at all the various stages with the same interest and enthusiasm as when one began. Burnout is a common problem in all professions, and it is perhaps worse when one chooses a career which offers relatively modest financial rewards and which the larger, popular culture does not deem terribly important.

The most vital component in keeping enthusiasm alive and well is musical performance. Practicing or performing should come before everything else, including teaching! If one wishes to teach performance, one must experience performance in an ongoing way. Of course, any person who lives long enough will eventually reach a time when the physical means necessary to play may become diminished. I do not refer to this: rather, I am concerned about the hypocrisy of pretending to teach performance when the *desire* to perform has gone. The best way to keep such desire is by thoughtful, faithful practice of one's art. Such dedication and concern will be conveyed to one's students far more effectively than sermonizing about the importance of practicing.

Continued study is also important. I am always impressed by singers, pianists, and dancers who continue to study throughout their entire careers. One is never too old to benefit from the experience of a wise performer/teacher. New ideas or old ideas presented in new ways can provide the stimulation that we all need from time to time. Such continued study is *not* a sign of lack of knowledge or skill but is, rather, a sign of intelligence, continued enthusiasm, and a vital pursuit of one's art.

Reading, listening, and attending clinics or workshops can help to stimulate growth, avoid burnout, and keep one's focus. If such efforts are pursued relentlessly, a career as a university musician can be challenging and rewarding and a great way to practice one's art.

Sound and Intonation

This article appeared in the *ITG Journal*, Pedagogical Topics,
Jon Burgess, Editor (March 2003). Reprinted by permission.

There is a remarkably high degree of correlation between the quality of a player's sound and the accuracy of the player's intonation. I have rarely, if ever, heard a performer who produced a rich singing sound who played with poor Intonation. One hears both qualities done well or neither done well. The reasons for positive correlation between good sound and good intonation are two. Both good sound and good intonation require full, efficient production and highly developed aural skills. Time spent choosing a fine mouthpiece and trumpet, or working with a tuner is certainly time well spent, but these activities must never take the place of developing good tone production and good listening skills.

Many students are criticized for poor intonation and told to spend lots of time working with a tuner as a first step to playing better in tune. This approach fails to take into account the fact that the most that can be gained from using a tuner is to give the player a sense of the nature and extent of the pitch problem. The musician's ear must ultimately be changed (improved). Certainly, the use of a tuner is a positive technique, but the tuner might best be thought of as training wheels for the ear, not as the ultimate solution.

The most effective approach I have found in improving sound and intonation is to work with the student on good tone production. Good posture and full airflow (in both directions) are absolute necessities if any real quality is to be achieved. After the student has at least a rudimentary grasp of how to take and use air efficiently, I then have the student sing a simple line. The line must be well sung, i.e., using a rich tone quality and with excellent pitch. After this has been accomplished, I ask the student to play the line on the mouthpiece, thinking of the same musical qualities as in singing. Sound must be full and easy, and pitch must be accurate. (The student may play on the mouthpiece alone or with the mouthpiece inserted into a buzzing device attached to the trumpet. Either should work well). It is often helpful for the teacher to play the simple line on piano simultaneously so that the student has an immediate check on pitch.

Only after this process of working on breathing, singing, and mouthpiece playing has been done well will the student be asked to play the line on the trumpet. What this approach teaches the student, at the most basic level, is that he or she is entirely responsible for the quality of the sound and the excellence of the pitch. The equipment may be of some help, but it must never be depended upon to do the player's job. Sound always comes *from the player* through the trumpet, not from the trumpet.

This four-stage process of breathing, singing, playing on the mouthpiece, and playing on the trumpet is simple and effective. If any of the last three levels is less than fully successful, the player should return to the previous level and make certain it is performed with excellence. Perhaps the greatest value of this approach is that it deals with making music at the most fundamental levels. Good breathing and good listening can be applied successfully with all musical phrases from the simple to the complex.

Endnotes

1. Keith Johnson, interview by Trevor Duell, February 15, 2014.
2. Ibid.
3. Ibid.
4. Ibid.
5. Ibid.
6. Ibid.
7. Ibid.
8. Ibid.
9. Ibid.
10. Ibid.
11. Ibid.
12. Ibid.
13. Ibid.
14. David Loucky, conversation with author, November 3, 2019.
15. Kristin Van Cleve, email to author, November 15, 2019.
16. Keith Johnson, letter to friends and family, August 18, 2013.
17. Johnson, interview by Duell.
18. Nicholas Daugherty, email to author, July 23, 2019.
19. Dave Monette, email to author, December 9, 2019.
20. Johnson, interview by Duell.
21. Thomas Tritle, email to author, October 21, 2019.
22. Donald Little, email to author, January 19, 2020.
23. Jon Hansen, email to author, October 14, 2019.
24. Tritle, email.
25. Donald Little, conversation with author, November 4, 2019.
26. Johnson, interview by Duell.
27. Mark Duffy, email to author, October 28, 2019.
28. Nicholas Daugherty, email to author, July 23, 2019.
29. Ibid.
30. Johnson, interview by Duell.
31. Jesse Eschbach, email to author, November 3, 2019.
32. Little, conversation.
33. Numbers averaged from Keith Johnson's annual College of Music "Updates," 2003–2011.
34. Keith Johnson, "Update," 2003.

35. Keith Johnson, "Update," 2004.

36. Keith Johnson, "Update," 2005.

37. Dr. John Scott, conversation with author, November 1, 2019.

38. Susan Rider, email to author, August 17, 2019.

39. Trevor Duell, email to author, September 30, 2019.

40. Anne Hardin, conversation with the author, September 14, 2020.

41. Brian Shook, email to the author, September 17, 2020.

42. Annette Hammett Talley, email to author, September 21, 2020.

43. Marc Reed, email to author, October 28, 2019.

44. Jason Dovel, email to author, August 28, 2019.

45. Kurt Gorman, email to author, July 27, 2020.

46. Dovel, email.

47. James Wood, email to author, November 24, 2019.

48. Eric Swisher, email to author, August 5, 2019.

49. Calvin Hofer, email to author, July 30, 2019.

50. Ward Yager, email to author, August 1, 2019.

51. David Spencer, email to author, November 22, 2019.

52. Etienne Stoupy, email to author, December 7, 2019.

53. Raquel Samayoa, email to author, November 1, 2019.

54. Johnson, interview by Duell.

55. Keith Johnson, conversation with author, April 28, 1990.

56. Ibid.

57. Johnson, interview by Duell.

58. Keith Johnson, "Why I Teach," *North Texan*, June 13, 2013.

59. Steve Leisring, email to author, October 3, 2019.

60. Reed, email.

61. Swisher, email.

62. Jason Dovel, email to author, August 28, 2019.

63. Larry Wells, email to author, July 25, 2019.

64. William Stowman, email to author, July 31, 2020.

65. Reed, email.

66. Keith Benjamin, email to author, July 21, 2019.

67. Spencer, email.

68. Stoupy, email.

69. John Cord, email to author, July 25, 2019.

70. Jason Bergman, email to author, November 1, 2019.

71. Edward Kleinhammer, *The Art of Trombone Playing* (Los Angeles: Summy- Birchard, 1963).

72. Jean-Baptiste Arban, *Arban's Complete Conservatory Method for Trumpet* (New York: Carl Fischer, 1982).

73. Keith Johnson, *The Art of Trumpet Playing* (Ames, IA: Iowa State University Press, 1981).

74. Keith Johnson, "Braces and the Young Trumpet Student," *Getzen Gazette*, December 1987.

75. Philip Farkas, *The Art of Brass Playing* (Anniston, AL: Wind Music, 1962).

76. Stewart Ross, "An Interview with Frank Crisafulli," *The Instrumentalist* 32, no. 3 (October 1977).

77. Pat Harbison, *Technical Studies for the Modern Trumpet* (Van Nuys, CA: Alfred Music, 2015).

78. James Stamp, *Warm-Ups and Studies for Trumpet* (Vuarmarens, Switzerland: Editions BIM, 1981).

79. Frank Wilson, M.D., *Mind, Muscle, and Music: Physiological Clues to Better Teaching* (Elkhart, IN: Selmer, 1981).

80. Keith Johnson, *Progressive Studies for the High Register* (Denton, TX: Harold Gore, 1991).

81. Keith Johnson, "Basic Skills for Young Trumpeters," *The School Musician*, June 1983.

82. Keith Johnson, *Brass Performance and Pedagogy*. (Upper Saddle River, NJ: Pearson, 2002).

Written Works and Discography of Keith Johnson

Books

The Art of Trumpet Playing. Denton, TX: Harold Gore, 1995. First published 1981 by Iowa State University Press.

Brass Performance and Pedagogy. Upper Saddle River, NJ: Pearson, 2002.

Articles

"The Brass Quintet in the High School." *Iowa Bandmaster's Magazine*, Winter 1969.

"The Brass Quartet in the High School." *Iowa Bandmaster's Magazine*, Fall 1971.

"Selected Contest Literature for Trumpet." *Iowa Bandmaster's Magazine*, Winter 1972.

"Choosing a Trumpet Mouthpiece." *Getzen Gazette*, December 1975. First published in *Iowa Bandmaster's Magazine*, Winter 1974.

"Intonation on the Trumpet." *Iowa Bandmaster's Magazine*, Winter 1976.

"Playing the Piccolo Trumpet." *National Association of College Wind and Percussion Instructors Journal*, Fall 1978.

"The Cornet Today." *The Instrumentalist*, April 1978.

"Playing the Fluegelhorn." *Getzen Gazette*, September 1978.

"Pedal Tones." *Getzen Gazette*, April 1979.

"Choosing a Trumpet." *Iowa Bandmaster's Magazine*, Fall 1980.

"Changing Trumpet Mouthpieces." *Getzen Gazette*, Spring 1981.

"Playing Trumpets in Various Keys." *Getzen Gazette*, Spring 1981.

"Teaching the Art of Listening." *International Trumpet Guild Journal*, October 1981.

"The Trumpet Warm-up." *Getzen Gazette*, September 1982.

"Teaching the Young Brass Player." *North Carolina Music Educator*, Fall 1982.

"Advantages of the Cornet for the Beginning Student." *Getzen Gazette*, 1982.

"The Upper Register for the Trumpet." *Getzen Gazette*, January 1983.

"Basic Skills for Young Trumpeters." *The School Musician*, June 1983.

"The View from the Best Seat in the House." *Bravo Magazine*, February/ March 1984

"Listening: A Guide to Better Trumpet Performance." *Getzen Gazette, 1985.*

"An Interview with Robert King." *International Trumpet Guild Journal*, September 1985.

"Taking Auditions." *Getzen Gazette*, April 1987.

"Braces and the Young Trumpet Student." *Getzen Gazette*, December 1987.

"Performance Anxiety." *Southwestern Musician*, December 1987.

"Finding the Right Trumpet." *Band World*, November, 1989. First published in *Getzen Gazette*, April 1988.

"The Right Trumpet for the Job." *Getzen Gazette*, April 1989.

"Cornet or Trumpet." *Southwestern Musician*, February 1990.

"Teaching the Beginning Cornet Student." *Southwestern Musician*, April 1990.

"Good Respiratory Practices for Brass Performers." *International Trumpet Guild Journal*, May 1990.

"The Monette Mouthpiece." *Monette*, Summer 1990.

"Teaching the Young Orchestral Trumpet Player." *Southwestern Musician*, December 1990.

"Articulation (Part I, Single Tonguing)" and "Articulation (Part II, Multiple Tonguing)." *Getzen Gazette*, Fall 1991.

"The University Musician." *International Trumpet Guild Journal*, May 1994.

"Intonation." *The DEG Report*, Fall 2001.

"Sound and Intonation." *International Trumpet Guild Journal*, January 2003.

"Vincent Cichowicz: A Remembrance." *International Trumpet Guild Journal*, March 2007.

"Listening: The Primary Musical Skill." *International Trumpet Guild Journal*, Online, http//www.trumpetguild.org.), January 2010. https://www. trumpetguild.org/images/ITGYouth/Masterclass/keithjohnson.pdf.

Co-Authored Articles

"A Review of Brass Quintets." (with members of the Northern Brass Quintet: Bruce Chidester, Gordon Halberg, Jon Hansen, David Kennedy) *National Association of College Wind and Percussion Instructors Journal*, Spring 1971.

"A Graded List of Brass Ensembles for School Use." (with Bruce Chidester) Iowa *Bandmaster's Magazine*, Fall 1979.

Chapters

"Keith Johnson." In *Arnold Jacobs: The Legacy of a Master: The Personal and Pedagogical Recollections of Thirty-one of His Colleagues, Students, and Friends*. Compiled by M. Dee Stewart. Evanston, IL: The Instrumentalist Publishing Co., 1987.

Method Books

Progressive Studies for the High Register. Denton, TX: Harold Gore, 1991. (Editions for trumpet, horn, trombone, and tuba)
Method for Baroque Trumpet. Unpublished manuscript.

Editions

Duets by Thomas Morley. Transcribed by Leigh Anne Hunsaker and edited by Keith Johnson. Denton, TX: Harold Gore, 1992. (Editions for trumpet, horn, trombone, and tuba)

Unpublished Compositions

"For Whom the Bell Tolls." Soprano and piano. Composed for Phi Mu Alpha initiation, 1961.
Mass of the Blessed Virgin Mary. Voices and organ. Composed for the baptism of Andrea Johnson, 1976.
St. Luke's Mass. Voices and organ. Composed for the baptism of Stephen Johnson, 1978.
St. Augustine's Mass. Voices and organ. Composed for Reverend William Hubbell's birthday, 1980.
"The Donkey." Text by G. K. Chesterton. Children's voices and keyboard. Written for Cecile Johnson and the Woodrow Wilson All Star Choir, 1990.

Discography

Symphony of Psalms. Margaret Hills, conductor, Interlochen Records, 1963.
Contemporary American Brass Quintet. The Northern Brass Quintet, n.d.

Of Men and Mountains. The New Hampshire Music Festival Orchestra, Tom Nee, conductor. Hamer Records, 1979.

The Choir of Highland Park Presbyterian Church. David Davidson, conductor, private issue, 1988.

Choral Music from Highland Park Presbyterian Church, David Davidson, conductor, private issue, 1989.

Gustav Mahler's Symphony No. 2. The Dallas Symphony Orchestra, Eduardo Mata, conductor, Telarc, 1990.

Hark! A Thrilling Voice Is Calling – Christmas at the Church of the Incarnation, Dallas, TX, Kevin Clarke, conductor, and the Sundance Brass Ensemble, 2001)

Music of Jonathon Willcocks: A recording of contemporary settings by the Southwest Seminary Chorale, C. David Keith, conductor, and the Sundance Brass Ensemble, n.d.

Music for Christmas: A recording of seasonal music for choir and brass by the Sundance Brass Ensemble and the Southwest Seminary Choir, n.d.

Facets: Music for Solo and Multiple Trumpets. John Holt, solo trumpet, and trumpet ensemble. Crystal Records, CD762, 2004.

UN*conventional Trumpet:* John Holt, trumpet, with Keith Johnson; Natalia Bolshakova, piano. Crystal Records, CD 763, 2004.

Associates Contributing Remembrances

Keith Benjamin, Bachelor of Music Education, Morningside College, 1982; Master of Music, University of Northern Iowa, 1984; DMA with Performer's Certificate, Eastman School of Music, 1989. Curator's Professor of Trumpet, University of Missouri-Kansas City Conservatory of Music and Dance, 1989–present.

Jason Bergman, Bachelor of Music, Brigham Young University, 2006; Master of Music, University of Michigan, 2008; DMA, University of Michigan, 2011. Associate professor of trumpet, University of North Texas, 2015–2018; associate professor of trumpet, Brigham Young University, 2018–present.

John Cord, Bachelor of Music, University of Iowa, 2002; Master of Musical Arts, Yale University School of Music, 2004; DMA, University of North Texas, 2009. Associate professor of music, Luther College, 2013–present. Member, La Crosse (WI) and Waterloo-Cedar Falls (IA) symphony orchestras.

Nicholas Daugherty, Bachelor of Arts in Music Education, University of Northern Iowa, 1987; Master of Science in Education, Drake University, 1991. Director of bands, John Adams Middle School, Mason City, 1989–2003; Worship Pastor, 2003–2012; Executive Pastor, Grace Church, 2012–present.

Jason Dovel, Bachelor of Music, James Madison University, 2003; Master of Music, Bowling Green State University, 2005; DMA, University of North Texas, 2007. Associate professor of trumpet, University of Kentucky, 2013–present; Director, UK Summer Trumpet Institute; Board of Directors, the Historic Brass Society and the International Trumpet Guild.

Trevor Duell, Bachelor of Music Education, Bachelor of Music, Fort Hays State University, 2008; Master of Music, Lamar University, 2011; DMA,

University of North Texas, 2016. Specialist Musician/Sgt., U.S. Army Band, 2017–present.

Mark Duffy, Bachelor of Arts, University of Northern Iowa, 1987. Sales Manager at Rieman Music, Des Moines, IA. Has performed in ensembles from the Waterloo-Cedar Falls Symphony Orchestra to Jah Blue Oasis, Knee Deep, The Rock Farmers, Riddle Me This, and most recently, Ampex Dementor.

Jesse Eschbach, Bachelor of Music, 1973, Master of Music, Indiana University, 1975; DMA, University of Michigan, 1980. Professor of organ, University of North Texas, 1986–present.

Jonas Feldman, Bachelor of Music, University of North Texas, 2000; Master of Music, San Francisco Conservatory, 2003. Member, Royal Canadian Artillery Band.

Adam Gordon, Bachelor of Music, University of Southern California, 1977; Master of Music, San Francisco Conservatory of Music, 1985. Senior lecturer of trumpet, University of North Texas; former assistant principal trumpet, Fort Worth Symphony. Baroque trumpet soloist and clinician.

Kurt Gorman, Bachelor of Arts, University of Chicago, 1994; Master of Music, University of North Texas, 1996; DMA, University of Missouri, Kansas City, 2001. Professor of music, University of Tennessee at Martin, 2004–present. Principal trumpet, Paducah Symphony Orchestra, 2013–present.

Allison Davis Hamlett, Bachelor of Arts in Music, University of North Texas, 2001; Master of Business Administration and Arts Administration, Southern Methodist University, 2003.

Jon Hansen, Bachelor of Arts, 1961, and Master of Arts, University of Northern Iowa, 1965. Professor of trombone, University of Northern Iowa, 1969–1993; Professor emeritus of trombone, University of Northern Iowa, 1993–present.

John Harbaugh, Bachelor of Arts in Music Education, University of Northern Iowa, 1975; Master of Music Education, North Texas State University, 1997. Professor of music, Central Washington University, 2002–present.

Anne Hardin, Bachelor of Music, Georgia State University, 1976; Master of Music Education with performance certificate, University of South Carolina, 1978; Ph.D., Music Education, University of South Carolina, 1990. Editor, *International Trumpet Guild Journal*, 1978–1996. Music educator, 1978–2004. Author, *A Ray Bradbury Compendium*, Polaris Press.

Calvin Hofer, Bachelor of Arts, South Dakota State University, 1985; Master of Music Education, University of Wisconsin, 1991; DMA, University of North Texas, 2000. Director of bands and former professor of trumpet, Colorado Mesa University; Head, Department of Music, Colorado Mesa University, 2004–2019; NASM representative, 2019–present.

Michael Laird, Academy of St. Martin-in-the-Fields, Academy of Ancient Music, English Concert. Chamber music recordings include *Brandenburg Concerto No. 2* with The English Concert and Trevor Pinnock, conductor, as well as first video performance of Handel aria, "The Trumpet Shall Sound," on period instruments with Academy of Ancient Music, Sir Christopher Hogwood, conductor. Fellow, Royal College of Music, 1993; professor (retired), Royal College of Music, 1982–95.

Steve Leisring, Bachelor of Music Education, 1986, and Bachelor of Music in trumpet performance, University of North Texas, 1987; Master of Music in trumpet performance, Mannes College of Music, 1989. Tenerife (Spain) Symphony Orchestra, 1989–2003. Professor of trumpet, University of Kansas, 2003–present.

Donald Little, Bachelor of Music Education, Peabody Conservatory, 1970; Master of Music, Northwestern University, 1971. Former professor of music, University of Northern Iowa, 1973–76; professor of tuba, University of North Texas, 1976–present. Principal tuba, Fort Worth Symphony, 1980–2001; principal tuba and cimbasso, Dallas Opera Orchestra 1988–2012.

Nathan Little, Bachelor of Music, Baylor University, 1990; Master of Music, University of North Texas, 2021. Principal trumpet, Las Colinas Symphony Orchestra, 2018–present.

David Loucky, Bachelor of Arts, Wesleyan University, 1982; Master of Music, Yale University, 1984; DMA, SUNY Stony Brook, 1987. Professor of music (trombone), Middle Tennessee State University, 1989–present. Member, New Hampshire Music Festival Orchestra, 1987–present.

Mark Lynn, Bachelor of Music, University of Louisville, 2005; Master of Music, University of Memphis, 2007; DMA, University of North Texas, 2010; Master of Business Administration, University of Dayton. Instructor of trumpet, assistant director of bands, University of Louisville, 2011–2016. Vice President of Operations, Dr. Mark Lynn & Associates PLLC, 2016–present.

Ann MacMillan, Bachelor of Music Education, Emporia State University, 1989; Master of Music Education, University of North Texas, 1995. Repair technician and instructor, University of North Texas, 1997–present.

Scott Meredith, Bachelor of Music Education, Bachelor of Music, University of Northern Colorado, 1996; Master of Music, University of North Texas, 2002; DMA, University of North Texas, 2008. Associate professor of music, University of Wyoming, 2008–2019. Principal trumpet, Port Angeles Symphony (Seattle), 2019–present.

Dave Monette, owner of David G. Monette Corporation, Portland, Oregon. Designer of custom brass instruments and mouthpieces.

Rob Murray, Bachelor of Music Education, University of Washington, 1983; Bachelor of Music, Portland State University, 1994; MST in Music, Portland State University, 1996; DMA, University of North Texas, 2002. Professor of trumpet, Columbus State University, 2009–present; principal trumpet, North Charleston POPS!; Archivist, International Trumpet Guild, 2014–present.

Marc Reed, Bachelor of Music Education, Bachelor of Music, Drake University, 2002; Master of Music, 2004, DMA, University of North Texas, 2007. Director, Schools of Music and Dance, Theatre, and Arts Administration, University of Akron, 2019–present.

Susan Rider, Bachelor of Music, University of Northern Iowa, 1989; Master of Music, Indiana University, 1991; Doctor of Music in Brass

Pedagogy, Indiana University, 2000. Member, trumpet/cornet section, "The President's Own" United States Marine Band, Washington, DC, 1997–present.

Raquel Rodriquez Samayoa, Bachelor of Music, West Texas A&M University, 2000; Master of Arts, West Texas A&M University, 2001; DMA, University of North Texas, 2008. Assistant professor of trumpet, University of North Texas; co-conductor, UNT Brass Band, Lantana Trio, Seraph Brass, 2018–present.

John Scott, Bachelor of Science in Music Education, Frostburg State University, 1969; Master of Music, 1971, and Doctor of Music in performance woodwinds and music literature, Indiana University, 1982. Professor of music, 1981–2018, professor emeritus of clarinet, University of North Texas. Former chair of the Division of Instrumental Studies and Associate Dean for Admissions, University of North Texas.

Brian Shook, Bachelor of Music, Cedarville University, 2001; Master of Music, 2003; DMA, 2006, Arizona State University. Chair, Mary Morgan Moore Department of Music, Lamar University (Beaumont, TX). Author, *Last Stop, Carnegie Hall: New York Philharmonic Trumpeter William Vacchiano*, UNT Press, 2011.

David Spencer, Bachelor of Music Education, Florida State University, 1986; Master of Music, University of North Texas, 1989; DMA, University of North Texas, 2002. Associate professor of music, University of Memphis, 1993–present.

Etienne Stoupy, Undergraduate degree, Conservatoire de Lyon (France), 2005; Master of Music, University of Memphis, 2007; DMA, University of North Texas, 2011. Assistant band director, S. J. Welsh Middle School, and current assistant principal trumpet, Acadiana Symphony Orchestra, 2017–present.

William Stowman, Bachelor of Science in Music Education, Indiana University of Pennsylvania, 1985; Master of Music Education (1992) and Master of Music in Performance (1993), Eastern Kentucky University; DMA,

University of North Texas, 1998. Professor of trumpet, Messiah University, 1996–present.

Eric Swisher, Bachelor of Music Education, University of Oklahoma, 1994; Master of Music, Indiana University, 1997; DMA, University of North Texas, 2006. Professor of trumpet, Murray State University, 2003–present.

Annette Hammett Talley, Bachelor of Music Education, University of North Texas, 2002; Master of Music Education, University of Central Oklahoma, 2012. Former teacher, band, choir, and humanities, Malawi, Africa and Jones, Oklahoma. Current teacher, Epic Charter Schools.

John Thiessen, Bachelor of Music, Eastman School of Music, 1987; Master of Music, historical musicology, King's College, 1990. Performer, Philharmonia Baroque Orchestra, Trinity Baroque Orchestra, and Tafelmusik. Faculty member in historical performance, The Juilliard School, 2009–present.

Thomas Tritle, Bachelor of Music, Baldwin-Wallace College Conservatory, 1970; Master of Music, New England Conservatory, 1975; DMA, University of Iowa, 1986. Professor of music, University of Northern Iowa, 1980–2006; principal horn, Waterloo/Cedar Falls Symphony Orchestra, 1980–2004.

Kristin Van Cleve, Bachelor of Music, 1987, and Master of Music in violin performance, University of North Texas, 1989. Chair, University of Dallas Department of Music, 2011–present. Principal violinist, Texas Camerata, 1990–present; principal second violin, Dallas Opera Orchestra, 2005–present; New Hampshire Music Festival Orchestra, 2003–present.

Larry Wells, Bachelor of Arts, music, Bachelor of Science, Education, Washington State University, 1990; Master of Science, Portland State University, 1996; DMA, University of North Texas, 2006. Director of Instrumental Studies, Methodist University, Fayetteville, NC, 2006–present; member, Fayetteville Symphony and Carolina Philharmonic; music director, Fayetteville Youth Symphony.

James Wood, Bachelor of Music, New England Conservatory, 1993; Master of Music, Northwestern University, 1994; DMA, University of North Texas, 2007. Member, U.S. Army Field Band, 2001–present; Auditions Coordinator and Administration Group Leader, 2014–present.

Ward Yager, Bachelor of Music Education, University of Memphis, 2001; Master of Music, University of North Texas, 2004; DMA, University of Maryland, 2014. Master Sergeant, U.S. Army Field Band, 2004–present.

Index